Especially for

....

From

....

Date

....

The 12 Days of Christmas
COOKBOOK

The Ultimate in Effortless Holiday Entertaining

BARBOUR BOOKS
An Imprint of Barbour Publishing, Inc.

Written and compiled by Nanette Anderson in association with Snapdragon Group℠.

ISBN 978-1-63409-023-0

Published by Barbour Books, an imprint of Barbour Publishing, Inc., P.O. Box 719, Uhrichsville, Ohio, 44683, www.barbourbooks.com.

Our mission is to publish and distribute inspirational products offering exceptional value and biblical encouragement to the masses.

 Member of the
Evangelical Christian
Publishers Association

Printed in China.

Contents

Introduction

On the first day of Christmas my true love sent to me. . .

The Christmas season is a time for fellowship with family and friends, reaching out to strangers, celebrating traditions, and making memories. It's also a time when food becomes more than food—even common recipes take on a magical quality. The recipes in this book were chosen because they warm and inspire. They are easy to make and easy to share. We hope you will see the magic in each and every one as you move tastefully through your holiday season!

Father God, as we celebrate Christmas with all the joyful traditions that make this time of year so special, may we also give praise for the gift of Your Son, Jesus, who was born to redeem us. Amen.

On the first day of Christmas my true love sent to me. . .

An Appetizer on a Platter

Christmas is a season
for kindling the fire
for hospitality in the hall,
the genial flame of
charity in the heart.

WASHINGTON IRVING

Jesus, You were born to give us abundant life.
How we thank You, Lord, and savor Your
goodness in all things. Help us during
this joyous season to contemplate the rich
blessings of salvation and eternal life that
are Your incomparable gifts to us!

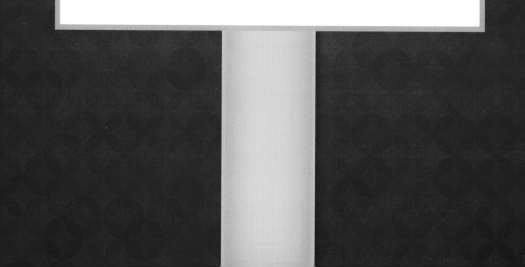

Be kindly affectionate to one
another. . .given to hospitality.

ROMANS 12:10, 13 NKJV

Toasted Tortilla Chips with Mango Salsa

CHIPS:

1 dozen flour tortillas

Vegetable oil

Salt

SALSA:

2 ripe mangos, peeled and diced; or 26-ounce jar mango slices, diced

1 medium red bell pepper, diced

1 jalapeño pepper, seeded and diced

3 tablespoons chopped fresh cilantro

2 tablespoons chopped fresh mint

1 small red onion, chopped

2 tablespoons honey

1 tablespoon lime juice

½ teaspoon salt

¼ teaspoon ground red pepper

Brush top side of each tortilla with oil. Cut into 8 wedges and spread on parchment-lined baking sheet. Sprinkle with salt. Bake at 375 degrees for 10 to 15 minutes or until crispy brown. For salsa, mix together all ingredients, cover, and chill for at least 2 hours.

YIELD: 4–6 SERVINGS

Deviled Eggs

6–7 hard-boiled eggs

¼ cup mayonnaise (more or less depending on desired consistency)

½ teaspoon spicy mustard

1 tablespoon dried minced onion

¼ teaspoon garlic salt

¼ teaspoon seasoned or regular salt

¼ teaspoon celery salt

¼ teaspoon pepper

¼ teaspoon paprika

12–14 sliced olives or pimento pieces for garnish

Carefully peel cooled eggs and slice lengthwise. Pop out yolks into small mixing bowl and arrange whites on plate. Mash yolks together with remaining ingredients until well blended. Pipe or spoon into whites. Garnish each with sliced olives or pimento pieces.

YIELD: 12–14 SERVINGS

Valentine's Dinner
Dance Menu

Vegetable Soup
Cranberry Garden Salad
Baked Chicken
Coleslaw
Baked Potato with Sour Cream and Butter
Green Beans with Roasted Carrots

Cheesecake with Cherry Topping

Four-Cheese Ball

1 small jar pimento cheese spread

1 small jar Old English spread

½ cup crumbled blue cheese

1 (8 ounce) package cream cheese, softened

1 dozen green olives, chopped

2 teaspoons dried minced onion

¼ teaspoon cayenne pepper

1 dash each Worcestershire sauce and liquid smoke

Salt and pepper to taste

¼ cup chopped pecans

Bring all ingredients (except pecans) to room temperature. Mix well and refrigerate. When cool, shape into ball and roll in pecans. Serve with a variety of crackers.

YIELD: 1 LARGE CHEESE BALL

Party Pecans

1 egg white

1 teaspoon water

1 pound pecan halves

1 cup sugar

1 teaspoon cinnamon

1 teaspoon salt

In large bowl, whip egg white and water to froth. Add pecans and coat well. In separate bowl, combine sugar, cinnamon, and salt. Add to pecans, using fingers to make sure all are coated. Shake off excess sugar mixture and spread on foil-lined baking sheet. Bake at 225 degrees for 60 to 90 minutes, stirring every 15 minutes. Pecans will crisp up as they cool.

YIELD: 2 CUPS

Stuffed Mushrooms

4–5 slices bacon, fried crisp and crumbled

12 fresh sturdy mushroom caps, stems removed

12 (1 inch) cubes mozzarella cheese

Grated Parmesan cheese

Divide bacon into each mushroom cap cavity. Place mozzarella cube in each cap. Place under oven broiler for about 5 minutes or until cheese is soft. Remove and sprinkle with Parmesan. Serve hot.

YIELD: 12 MUSHROOMS

Cream Cheese Pinwheels

2 (8 ounce) packages cream cheese, softened

1 (4 ounce) can diced green chilies

1 (4 ounce) can chopped black olives

1 (2 ounce) jar diced pimentos

3–4 flour tortillas

Mix ingredients together and spread on tortillas. Roll up gently and slice. Serve chilled.

YIELD: ABOUT 2 DOZEN PINWHEELS

Christmas Tradition Gyozas

1 tube high-quality breakfast sausage

1 package chopped cabbage (about 3 cups)

2 green onions, snipped

1 teaspoon Worcestershire sauce

1 teaspoon each ginger, chopped garlic, salt, and pepper

1 package square wonton wrappers

Soy sauce and picante sauce

Mix sausage, veggies, Worcestershire sauce, and spices well. Lay out several wonton wrappers at a time. With your finger, slightly dampen edges with water. Place small amount of meat mixture in center of each wrapper. Fold each over to form triangles and pinch moistened edges together to close. Deep fry in hot oil for about 1 minute (5–6 gyozas should be float frying at one time); flip and fry other sides for another minute. Gyozas should be deep golden brown. Drain each batch well on paper towels. Eat hot, dipped in equal parts soy sauce and picante sauce.

YIELD: 50 GYOZAS

Spicy Guacamole

3 ripe avocados

1 ripe Roma tomato, chopped

1 tablespoon dried minced onion

1 teaspoon lemon juice

2 tablespoons picante sauce or salsa

½ teaspoon salt

½ teaspoon garlic powder

1 dash pepper

4 drops hot sauce

Peel and mash or cube avocado. Gently mix in remaining ingredients. Let stand for 15 minutes and serve at room temperature, or refrigerate and serve cold.

YIELD: 6 SERVINGS

Jalapeño Dill Dip

1 small jar dill pickles

1 jalapeño pepper, seeded (canned or fresh)

⅔ cup sugar

½ teaspoon salt

1 (4 ounce) block cream cheese

Mix first four ingredients in blender until fairly smooth. Pour over cream cheese and serve with crackers. Very spicy!

YIELD: 8–10 SERVINGS

Olive Crescents

1 tube refrigerated crescent rolls

½ cup grated Italian cheese (Romano, Parmesan, etc.)

2 dozen green olives

Separate dough along perforated triangles. Gently flatten each triangle with rolling pin and cut into 3 triangles. Sprinkle cheese on each triangle and place an olive in center. Roll up and bake at 350 degrees for about 8 minutes. Serve immediately!

YIELD: 24 CRESCENTS

Cranberry Pecan Spread

2 cups creamy cottage cheese

2 tablespoons sour cream

1 tablespoon brown sugar

½ cup chopped pecans, toasted

½ cup dried cranberries (such as Craisins)

1 teaspoon finely grated lemon peel

Combine first six ingredients and mix well. Chill and serve on crusty french bread slices.

YIELD: 2 CUPS

Cocktail Meatballs

1½ cups chili sauce

1 cup grape jelly

2 teaspoons mustard

½ teaspoon salt

1 egg, beaten

3 tablespoons fine bread crumbs

1 pound ground beef

Combine chili sauce, jelly, and mustard and pour into slow cooker. Cover on high while making meatballs. Work salt, egg, and bread crumbs into meat until well blended. Shape into bite-size meatballs. Place on baking sheet and bake at 400 degrees for 15 minutes. Drain fat and add meatballs to slow cooker. Stir gently to coat. Cook on low for 6 hours. Serve skewered on toothpicks.

YIELD: 2 DOZEN

Pita Poppers

1 cup mayonnaise

1 small onion, finely chopped

½ cup slivered almonds

1½ cups finely shredded cheddar cheese

½ pound bacon, fried crisp and crumbled

1 package pita bread, halved and cut into triangles (or use mini pita bites)

Combine first five ingredients. Spread on pita triangles and bake at 400 degrees for 8 to 10 minutes.

YIELD: 8 SERVINGS

Corn and Bacon Dip

1 (8 ounce) package cream cheese, softened

1¼ cups sour cream

1 teaspoon minced garlic

1 teaspoon hot sauce

1 cup white shoepeg corn

½ teaspoon salt

½ pound bacon, fried crisp and crumbled

Combine all ingredients except bacon; chill. When ready to serve, sprinkle crumbled bacon on top. Serve with warm corn or tortilla chips.

YIELD: 3 CUPS

Teriyaki Chicken Wings

½ cup soy sauce

½ cup pineapple juice

2 tablespoons minced garlic

1 tablespoon ginger

½ teaspoon salt

½ teaspoon white pepper

2 dozen chicken wings

Pineapple chunks for garnish

Mix first six ingredients; add chicken wings and marinate for several hours in refrigerator. Remove from sauce and place on foil-lined baking sheet. Bake at 375 degrees for 30 to 40 minutes. Serve with pineapple chunks on toothpicks.

YIELD: 24 WINGS

Bacon-Wrapped Water Chestnuts

1 pound bacon

2 (8 ounce) cans whole water
chestnuts

Teriyaki glaze

Cut bacon slices in half and fry until almost done but still limp enough to wrap around water chestnuts. Secure bacon to chestnuts with toothpick. Dip each into bowl of teriyaki glaze and place on foil-lined baking sheet. Bake at 400 degrees until dark and crispy. Watch carefully so they don't burn.

YIELD: 30 CHESTNUTS

Party Nibbles

2 cups toasted oats cereal

2 cups toasted corn squares cereal

2 cups pretzel sticks

1 cup shoestring potatoes

1 pound salted mixed nuts

3 tablespoons Worcestershire sauce

1 teaspoon garlic salt

1 teaspoon seasoned salt

½ teaspoon onion salt

1 pound butter, melted

In large bowl, toss together first five ingredients. Stir remaining seasonings into melted butter and pour over dry mixture, stirring well to coat. Spread onto parchment-lined baking sheets and bake at 250 degrees for 2 hours, stirring every half hour.

YIELD: 8 QUARTS

Fruit Dip

1 (8 ounce) package cream cheese, softened

¾ cup dark brown sugar

¼ cup white sugar

2 teaspoons vanilla

1 dash salt

Combine all ingredients and chill well. Serve with whole stemmed strawberries, apple or pear slices, or any other fruit hefty enough to dip.

YIELD: 1½ CUPS

Holiday Salsa

1 (28 ounce) can diced tomatoes

1 (2 ounce) can chopped black olives

1 (2 ounce) can diced green chilies

3 green onions, chopped

3 tablespoons olive oil

2 teaspoons hot sauce

1½ tablespoons red wine vinegar

½ teaspoon garlic salt

½ teaspoon pepper

Combine all ingredients in large bowl and mix well. Cover and refrigerate for several hours before serving with warm tortilla chips.

YIELD: 3 CUPS

Zesty Salmon Pâté

1 (8 ounce) package cream cheese, softened

2 tablespoons snipped parsley

2 teaspoons finely chopped green onion

1 teaspoon seasoned salt

¼ teaspoon garlic powder

1 teaspoon hot sauce

1 (8 ounce) can salmon, drained and flaked

Parsley stems or lemon slices for garnish

Combine all ingredients (except garnish) until well mixed. Pour into 2-cup mold of any design and refrigerate for several hours. Unmold and add garnish. Serve with crackers.

YIELD: 2 CUPS

On the second day of Christmas my true love sent to me. . .

Two Beverages a-Blending

Christmas. . .is not an external event
at all, but a piece of one's home
that one carries in one's heart.

FREYA STARK

Lord, our souls are parched and longing for You!
As the deer pants after the refreshment of the stream,
lead us each day to quench our thirst with the
pure living water of Your Word. Amen.

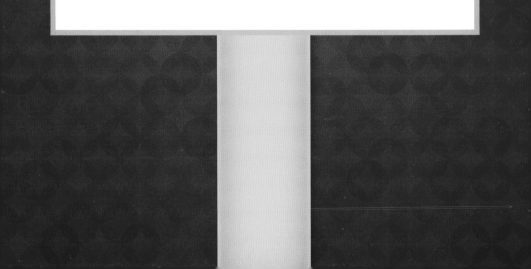

Whether you eat or drink or whatever you do,
do it all for the glory of God.

1 Corinthians 10:31 niv

Eggnog

4 cups cream

3 quarts whole milk

3 tablespoons cornstarch

8–12 eggs, separated

1½ cups sugar, divided

1 teaspoon salt

2 teaspoons nutmeg

4 teaspoons vanilla

3 teaspoons rum flavoring

8 drops yellow food coloring (optional)

Heat cream and milk together in large kettle, but pull from heat just before boiling. Dissolve cornstarch in 1 cup hot mixture and stir back into mixture in kettle. In large bowl, beat together egg yolks, 1 cup sugar, and salt. Blend with cooling milk mixture. In small bowl, stir nutmeg into ¼ cup sugar to prevent clumping and add to milk mixture along with vanilla and rum flavoring. Stir in food coloring if desired. In mixing bowl, beat egg whites with remaining ¼ cup sugar until fairly stiff; gently fold into milk mixture. Keep eggnog well refrigerated; serve cold.

YIELD: 1 GALLON

Hot Spiced Tea

6 cups water

1 teaspoon whole cloves

1 cinnamon stick

2 tablespoons loose black tea

1 cup orange juice

2 tablespoons lemon juice

¾ cup sugar

Combine water, cloves, and cinnamon stick in saucepan. Bring to boil and remove from heat. Add tea, stir, and cover. While tea steeps for 5 minutes, bring juices and sugar just to boil. Stir into hot tea and strain into cups.

YIELD: 6 CUPS

Pineapple Orange Fizzes

3 cups orange juice

1 (8 ounce) can crushed pineapple, with juice

1 glass crushed ice

Ginger ale

Blend first three ingredients until smooth. Fill serving glasses half full. Add cold ginger ale to fill each glass. Stir gently and serve.

YIELD: 6 CUPS

Golden Christmas Punch

1 (6 ounce) can frozen orange juice concentrate, thawed

1 (6 ounce) can frozen lemonade concentrate, thawed

16 ounces water

1 (12 ounce) can apricot nectar

2 cups pineapple juice

½ cup lemon juice

32 ounces ginger ale

Combine orange and lemonade concentrate with water. Add nectar, pineapple juice, and lemon juice; blend well. Chill. Just before serving, add cold ginger ale.

YIELD: 15 CUPS

Hot Cocoa Mix

5 cups instant dry milk

2½ cups powdered sugar

1 cup unsweetened cocoa powder

1 cup powdered nondairy creamer

1 teaspoon salt

In large bowl, combine all ingredients. Stir until thoroughly combined. Store in airtight container. For one serving, add ¼ cup cocoa mixture to ¾ cup boiling water and stir. Flavored nondairy creamers may be used to vary the taste!

YIELD: 12–15 CUPS

Wassail

3 quarts apple cider

2 cinnamon sticks

½ teaspoon nutmeg

½ cup honey

½ cup lemon juice

2 teaspoons finely grated lemon peel

5 cups pineapple juice

3 whole oranges

Whole cloves

Bring cider and cinnamon sticks to boil; reduce heat and simmer for 5 minutes. Add remaining ingredients (except oranges and cloves) and simmer 5 minutes longer, uncovered. Stud oranges with whole cloves and place in small baking pan with 2 tablespoons *water*. Bake at 325 degrees for 30 minutes. When ready to serve, float oranges in punch bowl with wassail. Remove cinnamon sticks or leave them to float with oranges. Wassail is best served warm.

YIELD: 20 CUPS

Down Under Christmas Smoothies

8 very ripe kiwi

2 teaspoons lime juice

½ cup raspberry liquid yogurt

1 cup lemonade

12 ounces cream soda or ginger ale

Peel kiwis and puree in blender with lime juice until smooth. Add yogurt and lemonade. Mix with sparkling soda to serve.

YIELD: 3–4 SMOOTHIES

Milk Punch

1 quart cold milk

46 ounces apricot juice

1 (6 ounce) can frozen pink lemonade concentrate, thawed

1 quart vanilla ice cream, softened

1 quart orange sherbet

1 quart ginger ale

Mix first five ingredients together in punch bowl. Add ginger ale last and stir gently.

YIELD: 16 CUPS

Choco-mint Cocoa

½ cup sugar

¼ cup instant cocoa mix

3 ounces dark chocolate chips

⅓ cup hot water

4 cups milk

1 teaspoon vanilla

¼ teaspoon peppermint extract

4 large peppermint candy canes, crushed

Mix sugar, cocoa mix, chocolate chips, and hot water in saucepan over medium heat, stirring continually until chocolate chips are melted. Add milk, vanilla, and peppermint extract. Stir until well blended and hot. Serve in mugs with sprinkling of crushed candy cane.

YIELD: 1½ QUARTS

Spicy Grape Punch

2 cups grape juice

½ cup sugar

1 cinnamon stick

1 teaspoon whole cloves

1 tablespoon lemon juice

1 (6 ounce) can frozen orange juice concentrate

1 cup water

Combine all ingredients in large saucepan and bring to boil. Remove cinnamon stick and cloves and serve hot.

YIELD: 8 CUPS

Minty Christmas Creams

* * *

2 cups crushed ice

4 ounces crème de cacao

2 ounces crème de menthe

6 generous scoops vanilla ice cream

Put all ingredients in blender and blend until well mixed.

YIELD: 4 CUPS

Double Lime Punch

* * *

2 cups lime sherbet, softened

1 (6 ounce) can frozen limeade concentrate, thawed

2 cups cold water

1 (2 liter) bottle ginger ale

Mix first 3 ingredients together in punch bowl. Add ginger ale last and stir gently.

YIELD: 12 CUPS

Peppermint Mocha Soda

Chocolate syrup

Club soda or ginger ale

Peppermint stick ice cream

Whipped cream for garnish

Maraschino cherries for garnish

For each soda, place 3 tablespoons chocolate syrup in tall glass. Fill glass half full with chilled club soda or ginger ale. Add 2 scoops peppermint stick ice cream and stir gently. Garnish with whipped cream and cherry.

Tomato Toddy

46 ounces tomato juice

46 ounces vegetable juice (such as V-8)

¾ cup sugar

15 whole cloves

4 cinnamon sticks

1 teaspoon salt

3 cups water

¼ cup lemon juice

1 teaspoon celery salt

1 teaspoon paprika

Simmer all ingredients for about 15 minutes. Remove whole spices and serve hot.

YIELD: 15 CUPS

Cranberry Spritzers

· · · · · · · ✦ · · · · · · · · · · · · · · ✦ · · · · · · · · · · · · · ✦ · · · · · · ·

1 quart cranberry juice cocktail   Ginger ale
2½ tablespoons lemon juice

Mix together first two ingredients. Fill serving glasses half full. Add cold ginger ale to fill each glass and stir gently.

YIELD: 4 SERVINGS

Russian Tea

2 cups orange Tang

1 cup sugar

1 envelope powdered lemonade mix

½ cup powdered instant tea

2 teaspoons cinnamon

1 teaspoon ground cloves

Blend all ingredients well and store in airtight container. For one serving, add 3 teaspoons tea mixture to 1 cup boiling water and stir. Decaf instant tea is now available, so you can enjoy Russian Tea in the evening, too!

YIELD: 15 CUPS

Pineapple Frost

2 cups pineapple juice

1 pint vanilla ice cream

2 tablespoons lemon juice

Put all ingredients in blender and blend until smooth.

YIELD: 4 SERVINGS

Cinnamon Cocoa

4 cups whole milk

1 cup chocolate syrup

1 teaspoon cinnamon

1 cup cream, whipped

¼ cup semisweet mini chocolate chips

Heat together milk and syrup in saucepan. Stir in cinnamon and serve in mugs. Garnish with whipped cream and chocolate chips.

YIELD: 5–6 CUPS

Party Punch Ring

1 small package lemon gelatin

1 cup hot water

2 cups cold water

2 cups sugar

46 ounces pineapple juice

1 (6 ounce) can frozen orange juice concentrate, thawed

2 liters ginger ale

Dissolve gelatin in 1 cup hot water. When completely dissolved, add remaining ingredients (except ginger ale) and mix well. Freeze in Bundt pan or ring mold of your choice. Set out to begin thawing 1 hour before serving. Unmold into empty punch bowl and add ginger ale. Ring will continue to thaw, releasing flavor into ginger ale as it melts. Keep adding ginger ale as punch gets low.

YIELD: 12–15 SERVINGS

Cranberry Apple Sippers

2 cups cranapple juice cocktail

½ cup whole milk

½ cup half-and-half

½ teaspoon nutmeg

¼ cup sugar

1 cup crushed ice

Put all ingredients in blender and blend until smooth.

YIELD: 3 CUPS

French Chocolate

1 cup semisweet chocolate chips

½ cup light corn syrup

¼ cup water

1 teaspoon vanilla

1 pint heavy cream

1 quart whole milk

Mix all ingredients in large saucepan and heat slowly, stirring constantly until chocolate chips are melted. A very rich chocolate drink to be served warm.

YIELD: 8–10 CUPS

On the third day of Christmas my true love sent to me. . .

Three Breads a-Rising

Unless we make Christmas an
occasion to share our blessings,
all the snow in Alaska
won't make it white.

BING CROSBY

You, Jesus, are the Bread of Life—
holy sustenance for starving souls.
You alone fill the hungry with good things.
Make us conscious, Father, of all those
around us who crave Living Bread! Amen.

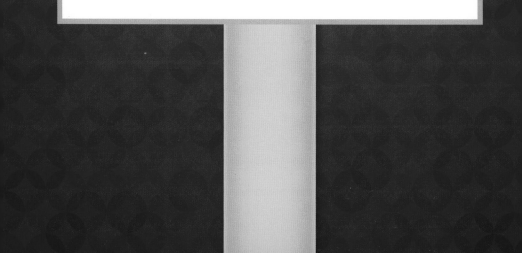

*"I am the living bread that came down from heaven.
Whoever eats this bread will live forever."*

JOHN 6:51 NIV

Zucchini Bread

2 cups flour

1 tablespoon cinnamon

2 teaspoon baking soda

1 teaspoon salt

¼ teaspoon baking powder

3 eggs

2 cups sugar

1 cup vegetable oil

2 cups unpeeled zucchini, coarsely grated and packed

½ cup raisins, tossed in flour

½ cup chopped nuts

In large mixing bowl, combine first five ingredients. In separate bowl, beat eggs, sugar, oil, and zucchini. Add to dry mixture and stir just until blended. Stir in floured raisins and nuts. Pour into two greased and floured loaf pans and bake at 350 degrees for 1 hour or until toothpick inserted in bread comes out clean.

YIELD: 2 LOAVES

Gingerbread

½ cup shortening

½ cup sugar

1 egg

1 cup molasses

2½ cups flour

1 teaspoon baking powder

½ teaspoon baking soda

½ teaspoon salt

1½ teaspoons ginger

1 teaspoon cinnamon

1 cup hot water

Whipped cream for garnish

In large bowl, cream together shortening, sugar, egg, and molasses. In separate bowl, combine flour, baking powder, baking soda, salt, ginger, and cinnamon. Add to creamed mixture along with hot water, mixing well. Pour into greased and floured 8x11-inch baking dish and bake at 350 degrees for 30 to 40 minutes. Put a dollop of whipped cream on each piece when serving.

YIELD: 10 SERVINGS

Ruth's Baking Powder Biscuits

2 cups flour

½ teaspoon salt

4 teaspoons baking powder

5 tablespoons shortening

¾ cup milk

Combine dry ingredients. Using fork, mix in shortening until dough is very crumbly. Add milk, stirring very little, just until blended. Turn out onto floured surface and gently pat to 1½ inches thick. Cut out biscuits with round cutter and place on ungreased baking sheet. Bake at 350 degrees for about 10 minutes or until slightly golden brown. Do not overbake!

YIELD: 7–8 BISCUITS

Aunt Annie's Banana Bread

3½ cups flour

2 cups sugar

1 cup vegetable oil

2 teaspoons vanilla

4 eggs, beaten

6 very ripe bananas, mashed

2 teaspoons baking soda

1 teaspoon salt

Combine all ingredients and bake in two greased and floured loaf pans. Bake at 350 degrees for 45 to 50 minutes.

YIELD: 2 LOAVES

Walnut Streusel Muffins

CRUMB MIXTURE:

2 cups flour

1½ cups brown sugar

¾ cup butter, softened

BATTER:

1 cup flour

2 teaspoons baking powder

1 teaspoon nutmeg

1 teaspoon cinnamon

¼ teaspoon ginger

½ teaspoon baking soda

½ teaspoon salt

¾ cup chopped walnuts, divided

1 cup buttermilk

2 eggs, beaten

Mix together crumb mixture ingredients just until blended. Measure out ¾ cup crumb mixture and combine with ¼ cup chopped walnuts. Set aside. Add remaining crumb mixture to batter ingredients. Mix well. Spoon into paper-lined muffin tins, filling two-thirds full. Top each muffin with spoonful of reserved crumb-nut mixture. Bake at 350 degrees for about 20 minutes.

YIELD: 1 DOZEN MUFFINS

Christmas Crescents

1 cup milk

7 tablespoons lard

1½ cakes yeast

½ cup sugar, divided

1 teaspoon salt

3 eggs, beaten

About 4 cups flour

½ cup butter, melted

Scald milk, but do not let it boil. Add lard, stirring until melted. Cool. In large mixing bowl, sprinkle 1 tablespoon sugar over yeast. Let rest 20 minutes. Meanwhile, add remaining sugar and salt to eggs. Add milk and yeast mixtures. Blend well. Begin adding flour, 2 cups to begin and then more as dough thickens. Cover and refrigerate overnight. Three hours ahead of serving, roll dough into three rounds, each ¼ inch thick. Brush with butter. Cut each round into 8 wedges like a pizza. Starting at wide end, roll each wedge into snug crescent. Brush with butter again and place on lightly greased baking sheets. Set aside for 2 hours to rise. Bake at 350 degrees for 8 minutes.

YIELD: 2 DOZEN

Sweet Corn Muffins

1½ cups flour

⅔ cup sugar

½ cup yellow cornmeal

1 tablespoon baking powder (yes, that's a tablespoon!)

½ teaspoon salt

2 eggs, lightly beaten

⅓ cup vegetable oil

3 tablespoons butter, softened

Combine dry ingredients and add to wet ingredients. Spoon into greased muffin tins. Bake at 350 degrees for 15 minutes. Allow to cool in pan before removing.

YIELD: 1 DOZEN

English Tea Scones

2 cups flour

1 teaspoon baking powder

¼ teaspoon salt

¼ cup sugar

½ cup cold butter

1 cup half-and-half

1 cup whipped cream and strawberry jam for garnish

Combine first four ingredients; cut in butter with fork or pastry blender until crumbly. Add half-and-half, very gently stirring together. The less this dough is handled, the better! Turn out onto floured surface and roll gently to 1½-inch thickness. Using knife, cut dough into 4- to 5-inch triangles and place on ungreased baking sheets. Bake at 350 degrees for 12 minutes. Serve with whipped cream and jam.

YIELD: 8 SCONES

Crusty Christmas Eve Bread

3 cups flour

1¾ teaspoons salt

½ teaspoon dry yeast

1½ cups water

Optional: dried cranberries, finely grated orange or lemon peel, chopped walnuts, cheese, spices, etc.

Before bed: In large mixing bowl, whisk together flour, salt, and yeast. Add water and work together until shaggy mixture forms. Cover bowl with plastic wrap and set aside overnight. In the morning, heat oven to 450 degrees. Place empty cast iron pot or stoneware dutch oven (with lid) in oven and heat for 30 minutes. Meanwhile, stir any optional add-ins into dough, turn out onto heavily floured surface, and shape into ball. Cover with plastic wrap and let sit while pot is heating. Remove hot pot from oven and drop in dough. Cover and return to oven for 30 minutes. Then remove lid and bake 15 minutes longer. Remove bread from pot and place on cooling rack to cool. This is a delicious, rustic, and very dense bread!

YIELD: 1 ROUND LOAF

Bran Rolls

2 packets dry yeast

1¼ cups warm water

1¼ cups shortening

1 cup whole bran

1 cup sugar

2 teaspoons salt

¾ cup boiling water

2 eggs, beaten

6–7 cups flour

Combine yeast with warm water and set aside. Mix together shortening, bran, sugar, and salt. Add boiling water and stir until shortening melts. Add 1 cup flour to help cool mixture; then add eggs and yeast. One cup at a time, add in remaining flour. Mix well and place in greased bowl. Cover and chill in refrigerator for up to two days. When ready to bake, form dough into balls that half fill a standard muffin cup. Let rise for 1 hour. Bake at 350 degrees for 15 to 20 minutes.

YIELD: 3 DOZEN

English Muffin Loaves

6 cups flour

2 packets dry yeast

½ teaspoon baking soda

2 teaspoons salt

1 tablespoon sugar

2 cups whole milk

½ cup water

Cornmeal

Combine flour, yeast, soda, salt, and sugar. Heat liquids in saucepan until warm and stir into dry mixture, blending well. Add more flour to mixture until dough is stiff enough to put into two greased loaf pans dusted generously with cornmeal. Sprinkle more cornmeal on top of each loaf and let rise about 1 hour. Bake at 375 degrees for 20 to 30 minutes.

YIELD: 2 LOAVES

Cranberry Nut Bread

2 cups flour

½ teaspoon salt

1½ teaspoons baking powder

1 cup sugar

2 teaspoons baking soda

2 tablespoons very warm water

1 egg, beaten

2 tablespoons butter, melted

½ cup orange juice

1 cup dried cranberries (such as Craisins)

½ cup chopped nuts

Combine first four ingredients in large bowl. Dissolve soda in warm water and add to flour mixture along with egg, butter, and orange juice. Gently stir in dried cranberries and nuts. Pour into large loaf pan and bake at 350 degrees for 1 hour.

YIELD: 1 LARGE LOAF

Apple Fritters

2 tart apples, peeled and coarsely chopped

2½ cups flour

¼ cup sugar

¼ cup brown sugar

1 tablespoon baking powder

1 teaspoon salt

1 teaspoon cinnamon

½ teaspoon nutmeg

2 eggs

3 tablespoons butter, melted

1 cup apple cider

GLAZE:

¼ cup butter, melted

1 cup powdered sugar

1 dash each salt and cinnamon

Apple cider

Combine first eight ingredients in large bowl, tossing until apples are completely coated. In separate bowl, beat together eggs, butter, and cider. Add to dry mixture and blend well. Using dutch oven or deep fryer, drop batter 1 tablespoon at a time into hot oil. Fry for about 4 minutes per side, pressing center gently with spoon to flatten fritter slightly and ensure it cooks all the way through. Drain on rack. When cool, combine first three glaze ingredients with enough cider to create glaze consistency. Brush onto fritters.

YIELD: 1 DOZEN FRITTERS

Holiday Corn Bread Stuffing

½ cup chopped onion

½ cup chopped green pepper

½ cup chopped celery

½ cup butter

2 teaspoons crushed sage

2 teaspoons salt

1 teaspoon pepper

2 cups unseasoned dried stuffing cubes

2 cups crumbled corn bread

1½ cups chicken or turkey broth

Sauté vegetables in butter until soft. Add sage, salt, and pepper and blend well. In large bowl, mix together stuffing cubes and corn bread. Add vegetable mixture and blend well, adding broth until mixture is thoroughly wet and spongy. Bake in large casserole dish at 350 degrees for 1 hour.

YIELD: 6 CUPS

Quick and Easy Coffee Cake

2 cups flour

1 teaspoon salt

4 teaspoons baking powder

2 eggs

1 cup sugar

1 cup whole milk or buttermilk

½ cup shortening, melted

TOPPING:

½ cup brown sugar

2 tablespoons flour

2 tablespoons butter, melted

¾ teaspoon cinnamon

¼ teaspoon nutmeg

Combine first three ingredients in large bowl. In separate bowl, mix together eggs, sugar, milk, and shortening. Add to dry ingredients and mix well. Pour half of batter into greased 9x13-inch pan. Mix together topping ingredients. Sprinkle half of topping mixture over batter. Repeat batter and topping layers. Bake at 350 degrees for 30 minutes.

YIELD: 12 SERVINGS

Apricot Bread

2 cups flour

½ cup brown sugar

1½ teaspoons baking soda

½ teaspoon nutmeg

½ teaspoon salt

1½ cups apple juice or cider

1 cup buttermilk

2 eggs, beaten

¼ cup vegetable oil

½ cup bran flakes cereal

½ cup chopped dried apricots

Combine first five ingredients in large bowl. In separate bowl, combine apple juice, buttermilk, eggs, and oil. Add to dry mixture. Fold in bran flakes and apricots. Pour into greased and floured large loaf pan and bake at 350 degrees for 45 to 50 minutes.

YIELD: 1 LARGE LOAF

Chester's Cheatin' Cheesy Biscuits

2 tubes refrigerated biscuits

Blue cheese crumbles or slices
of cheddar, swiss, or Muenster
cheese

Gently slice raw biscuits in half. Place one half of each on lightly greased baking sheet. Top with a few crumbles or slice of cheese. Cover with top half of biscuit dough and bake at 350 degrees for 12 to 15 minutes.

YIELD: 16 BISCUITS

Kranz

1 loaf frozen white dough

½ cup butter, softened

1 cup brown sugar

½ cup maraschino cherries, chopped

1 cup chopped pecans

Salt

2 tablespoons butter, melted

GLAZE:

1 cup powdered sugar

4 tablespoons butter, melted

¼ teaspoon vanilla

1 dash salt

Milk

Thaw frozen dough in plastic bag at room temperature until soft but not yet rising. Roll out into thin rectangle about 12 x 14 inches. Spread with butter, then brown sugar. Sprinkle with cherries and nuts. Sprinkle very lightly with salt. Roll up tightly, starting with long side, and pinch edges to seal. Bring ends together to form ring and pinch tightly together. Cover with damp towel and let rise for about 1 hour. (Should rise only slightly; don't let dough rise too much.) Brush with butter and bake at 350 degrees for 30 minutes. When cool, combine first four glaze ingredients with enough milk to make thick glaze. Pour over Kranz.

YIELD: 12 SERVINGS

Nutty Pumpkin Bread

3½ cups flour

2 teaspoons salt

1 teaspoon nutmeg

1 teaspoon cinnamon

3 cups sugar

2 teaspoons baking soda

2 cups canned prepared pumpkin

4 eggs, beaten

½ cup vegetable oil

½ cup butter, melted

1 cup milk

In large bowl, combine first six ingredients. In separate bowl, beat together pumpkin, eggs, oil, butter, and milk. Blend thoroughly with dry ingredients and pour into three greased and floured loaf pans, filling each two-thirds full. Bake at 350 degrees for 45 to 60 minutes or until knife inserted in center comes out clean.

YIELD: 3 LOAVES

Oatmeal Bread

1 cup buttermilk

1 cup rolled whole oats

1 egg, beaten

⅓ cup molasses or honey

4 tablespoons butter, melted

1 cup whole wheat flour

1 teaspoon baking soda

1 teaspoon salt

Optional: raisins, dried cranberries, or nuts

Stir buttermilk into oats. Let sit until oats are soft. Add remaining ingredients, adding fruit or nuts if you wish. Pour into large greased loaf pan. Bake at 350 degrees for about 1 hour.

YIELD: 1 LARGE LOAF

On the fourth day of Christmas my true love sent to me. . .

Four Breakfast Dishes a-Baking

Christmas is not a time nor a season,
but a state of mind. To cherish peace
and goodwill, to be plenteous in mercy,
is to have the real spirit of Christmas.

CALVIN COOLIDGE

Father in heaven, every
beautiful day begins with You!
Remind us that as we rested,
You were watching over us,
never sleeping, ever attentive.
Fill our waking hearts with
grateful prayer. Amen.

[The virtuous woman] gets up before dawn
to prepare breakfast for her household.

PROVERBS 31:15 NLT

Matchless Coconut Almond Granola

8 cups old-fashioned rolled oats

1 cup slivered or sliced almonds

1 cup unsweetened coconut shavings

½ cup raw sesame seeds

½ cup raw pumpkin seeds

½ cup raw sunflower seeds

¾ cup pure maple syrup

½ cup coconut oil

¼ cup honey

1 tablespoon molasses

1 tablespoon vanilla

2 teaspoons cinnamon

1 teaspoon sea salt

Combine oats, almonds, coconut shavings, and seeds in large mixing bowl. In separate bowl, stir together remaining ingredients and pour over dry ingredients. Mix well. Line two large jelly roll pans with parchment paper. Pour half of granola onto each sheet and spread evenly. Bake at 340 degrees for 12 minutes, toss granola gently, and continue baking at 325 degrees for 30 minutes longer, stirring every 10 minutes. Cool on baking sheets and store in airtight containers.

YIELD: 10 CUPS

Eggs in a Hole

----

2 tablespoons butter

2 thick slices bread

2 eggs

1 dash each salt, pepper, celery salt, and paprika

In large skillet, melt butter evenly. Using paring knife or biscuit cutter, cut 3-inch hole in middle of each slice of bread. Place slices side by side in pan. Over low heat, brown bread on first side and flip, moving it around to absorb remaining butter. Immediately crack 1 egg into each hole and add seasonings. Cook on medium heat until done.

YIELD: 2 SERVINGS

Crepes

----

3 eggs

1 cup milk

¾ cup flour

1 tablespoon sugar

½ teaspoon salt

3–4 tablespoons butter

Sweetened diced fruit

Whipped cream or syrup for garnish

Beat together eggs and milk. Stir in flour, sugar, and salt. For each crepe, melt 1 tablespoon butter in 8-inch skillet. When hot, pour 2 tablespoons batter into pan and tilt, spreading out batter to coat inside of pan. Flip to quickly cook other side. Turn out onto serving plate, fill with desired fruit and roll up. Top with whipped cream or syrup.

YIELD: 3–4 CREPES

Strawberry Ricotta Blintzes

4 crepes

1 quart fresh strawberries, sliced

1 cup ricotta cheese

2 tablespoons powdered sugar

1 cup heavy cream

1 tablespoon powdered sugar

Chocolate shavings (optional)

Prepare crepe recipe as instructed on previous page. In blender, puree 1 cup sliced berries. Add ricotta and 2 tablespoons powdered sugar, blending for only a few seconds. Place 2 generous tablespoons of mixture on each crepe, folding sides in and loosely rolling up. Place in buttered baking dish (crepes should be touching) and brush lightly with *butter*. Cover and bake at 325 degrees for 15 minutes. Combine cream with 1 tablespoon powdered sugar and stir to dissolve. Serve blintzes hot, topped with spoonful of berries and drizzle of cream. To add extra pizzazz, sprinkle chocolate shavings over blintzes just before serving.

YIELD: 4 SERVINGS

South-of-the-Border Breakfast Casserole

1 cup pork sausage

½ cup diced onions

¾ cup butter

6 slices bread, cubed

10 eggs

2½ cups whole milk

1 small can green chilies

1 teaspoon salt

1 teaspoon pepper

1½ cups shredded Mexican cheese blend

In large skillet, brown sausage and onions. Drain on paper towels. Add butter to pan and sauté bread cubes. Pour into casserole dish. In mixing bowl, beat together eggs, milk, green chilies, and spices until frothy. Pour half of mixture over bread, then add half of cheese. Repeat layers. Bake uncovered at 325 degrees for 45 minutes.

YIELD: 10 SERVINGS

Glazed Bacon

* * *

1 pound uncooked bacon

1 cup brown sugar

1 tablespoon Dijon mustard

2 tablespoons red wine

1 dash salt

Place bacon slices on foil-lined baking sheet. Bake at 350 degrees for about 15 minutes. Meanwhile, mix together sugar, mustard, wine, and salt. When bacon is almost crisp, drain off excess fat and pour half of glaze over bacon; return to oven. When well browned, turn bacon over and pour on remaining glaze. Cook 10 to 15 minutes longer or until golden brown. Immediately transfer to wax paper to cool.

YIELD: 6 SERVINGS

Eggs Florentine

* * *

3 thin baguette slices

1 (10 ounce) package frozen chopped spinach, thawed

3 eggs

3 ounces grated Parmesan cheese

Salt and pepper to taste

Preheat oven to 350 degrees. Place each baguette slice in bottom of individual baking dish. Squeeze excess moisture from spinach until almost dry. Divide among each dish on top of baguette. Carefully break egg over spinach and sprinkle with Parmesan, salt, and pepper. Bake for about 15 minutes or until egg whites are firm. Serve immediately.

YIELD: 3 SERVINGS

Cinnamon Raisin French Toast

- - - ★ - - - - - - ★ - - - - - ★ - - - -

6 eggs

½ cup heavy cream

1 teaspoon cinnamon

½ teaspoon salt

1 tablespoon butter

1 loaf unsliced raisin bread

Powdered sugar and whipped cream or syrup for garnish

Beat together eggs and cream just until well blended. Add cinnamon and salt. Melt butter in skillet. While heating, cut raisin bread into 2-inch slices. Dip each slice completely into egg mixture for a few seconds. Place in hot butter and brown on first side before flipping and browning top side. Sprinkle with powdered sugar and serve with whipped cream or syrup.

YIELD: 6 SERVINGS

Potato Pancakes (Latkes)

- - - ★ - - - - - - ★ - - - - - ★ - - - -

6 medium potatoes

1 small onion, chopped

2 eggs, beaten

3 tablespoons flour

½ teaspoon baking powder

1 teaspoon salt

½ teaspoon pepper

1 dash paprika

Peel and grate potatoes. Drain off any liquid and add remaining ingredients. Mix well and drop 1 tablespoon at a time onto hot, greased griddle. Brown both sides and drain on paper towels. Serve with sour cream, chives, shredded cheese, crumbled bacon, or sliced ham.

YIELD: 1 DOZEN LATKES

Buttermilk Biscuits and Red Eye Gravy

GRAVY:

- 16 ounces high-quality pork sausage
- 2 tablespoons flour
- 2 cups whole milk
- Salt and pepper to taste

BISCUITS:

- 2 cups flour
- ½ teaspoon salt
- 4 teaspoons baking powder
- ⅔ cup shortening
- ¾ cup milk
- 2 teaspoons sausage fat

Brown sausage in skillet; drain on paper towels. Reserve 2 tablespoons fat for biscuit preparation. Stir flour into skillet with remaining fat, gradually adding milk and heating until thick. Season with salt and pepper. For biscuits, combine flour, salt, and baking powder. Work shortening in with fork until mixture is coarse and crumbly; add milk, stirring just until moistened. Turn out onto lightly floured surface and pat down to 1-inch thickness. Cut into rounds. Pour reserved fat into shallow baking dish and top with biscuits. Bake at 375 degrees for 12 to 15 minutes.

YIELD: 4–6 SERVINGS

Energy Bars

½ cup butter, room temperature

1¼ cups brown sugar

6 cups old-fashioned rolled oats

1 cup raisins

1 cup dried cranberries (such as Craisins)

1½ cups chopped dried fruit: apricots, pineapple, cherries, etc.

2 teaspoons cinnamon

½ teaspoon nutmeg

1 teaspoon salt

⅔ cup vanilla or strawberry protein powder

⅔ cup flaxseed meal

1 cup salted peanuts

1 cup egg whites, from carton

1 cup natural peanut or almond butter

1 (14 ounce) can sweetened condensed milk

In large bowl, cut butter into brown sugar until coarse. Stir in oats, raisins, dried fruit, cinnamon, nutmeg, salt, protein powder, flaxseed meal, and peanuts. In separate bowl, combine egg whites, peanut butter, and condensed milk, whisking until smooth. Add to oat mixture and stir until well blended. Line two jelly roll pans with parchment and press mixture into them. Bake at 350 degrees for 20 minutes. Allow to cool in pans. Then grasp parchment at either end and lift slabs out onto hard surface. Cut into bars. These freeze well in snack-size ziplock bags.

YIELD: 3 DOZEN

Mexican Breakfast Pizza

1 tube refrigerated pizza crust
  dough

1 pound ham, cubed

1 cup chopped onion

1 teaspoon butter

6 eggs

2 tablespoons heavy cream

16 ounces fresh salsa

½ teaspoon salt

½ teaspoon pepper

1½ cups shredded Mexican cheese
  blend

Unroll dough and press into lightly greased pizza pan. Bake at 400 degrees
for 8 minutes. While crust cools, brown ham and onions together in
butter. Drain and set aside. Clean pan and lightly oil it. In mixing bowl,
beat eggs and mix in cream. Pour into pan and scramble. Spread salsa
on partially cooked pizza crust and top with ham, onions, and scrambled
eggs. Sprinkle with salt, pepper, and cheese. Return to oven and bake 10 to
12 minutes longer or until crust is golden brown and cheese is bubbly.

YIELD: 8 SMALL SLICES

Parfait Fruit Cups

1 cup granola

1 cup plain Greek yogurt

1 cup diced fruit or berries

In clear parfait glasses, layer ingredients twice in order given.

YIELD: 2 PARFAITS

Blueberry Pancakes

2 cups flour

2 teaspoons baking powder

½ teaspoon salt

1 egg, beaten

⅓ cup vegetable oil

1 cup buttermilk

1 tablespoon butter

1 cup blueberries

Combine dry ingredients. Stir in egg, oil, and buttermilk. If batter is too thick, add drop or two of water or regular milk to make good pancake batter consistency. Melt butter in skillet or on flat griddle. When very hot, pour two to three pancakes at a time, dotting with several blueberries. As air bubbles dot surface of batter, flip pancakes and cook about 1 minute longer.

YIELD: 15 PANCAKES

Easy Cinnamon Rolls

1 loaf frozen bread dough

½ cup butter softened

¾ cup brown sugar

½ cup chopped nuts

½ teaspoon salt

Cinnamon to taste

Thaw bread dough in plastic bag just until pliable. Roll out to ¼-inch thickness. Spread with butter. Sprinkle with brown sugar, nuts, salt, and cinnamon. Roll up tightly, starting with long side, and pinch edges to seal. Cut into 12 equal disks and place in greased baking pan. Cover and let rise for about 1 hour. Bake at 350 degrees for 20 minutes. To prevent rolls from sticking to pan, dump out onto wax paper immediately.

YIELD: 1 DOZEN CINNAMON ROLLS

Cheesy Grits Casserole

* * *

1 cup quick-cooking hominy grits

3 cups milk

1 teaspoon salt

¼ teaspoon pepper

2 eggs, beaten

1 cup water

6 tablespoons butter

1 cup shredded cheddar or
Monterey Jack cheese

1 small can chopped green chilies

In large saucepan, stir grits, milk, salt, and pepper together over medium heat, stirring often to prevent scorching. When thick, remove from heat and add eggs and water; mix until well blended. Return to burner and cook until thick again, stirring constantly. Mix in butter, cheese, and chilies. Spread in greased casserole dish and bake at 325 degrees for 30 minutes.

YIELD: 6 SERVINGS

Eggs Benedict with Blender Hollandaise Sauce

BLENDER HOLLANDAISE:

4 egg yolks

1 tablespoon lemon juice

1 dash each paprika, cayenne
pepper, and salt

¼ cup butter, melted

¼ cup extra virgin olive oil

EGGS:

Butter for greasing muffin tin

6 eggs

1 tablespoon water

Whisk egg yolks, lemon juice, seasonings, and butter until blended. Cook over very low heat, stirring constantly, until mixture starts to bubble. Remove from heat immediately and cool for 4 minutes. Pour into blender, cover, and blend on high speed while adding oil slowly in thin stream until sauce is thick and smooth. Scrape sides often. If making sauce ahead, refrigerate and warm over hot—not boiling—water while eggs are being prepared. Grease muffin cups with butter and crack 1 egg into each cup. Set muffin tin on jelly roll pan and pour water around tin's base. Bake at 350 degrees until set to your liking. Fork out onto individual plates and top with warm Hollandaise Sauce.

YIELD: 4 SERVINGS

Pear Breakfast Cake

¼ cup shortening

½ cup sugar

1 egg

½ teaspoon vanilla

1 cup flour

1 teaspoon baking powder

½ teaspoon baking soda

½ teaspoon salt

¼ teaspoon nutmeg

½ cup sour cream

¾ cup finely chopped ripe pear

TOPPING:

½ cup chopped walnuts

¼ cup brown sugar

½ teaspoon cinnamon

2 tablespoons melted butter

Cream together shortening, sugar, egg, and vanilla. In separate bowl, blend flour, baking powder, baking soda, salt, and nutmeg. Add to creamed mixture along with sour cream and pears. Pour into 8-inch square baking dish. Mix together topping ingredients until crumbly. Sprinkle over cake and bake at 350 degrees for 30 minutes.

YIELD: 6 SERVINGS

Oatmeal Muffins

1 cup flour

¼ cup sugar

3 teaspoons baking powder

½ teaspoon salt

¼ cup shortening

1 cup quick-cooking oats

1 cup milk

1 egg, beaten

Combine flour, sugar, baking powder, and salt. Cut in shortening until mixture is crumbly. Add oats and mix well. Gently stir in milk and egg. Spoon batter into greased muffin tin and bake at 400 degrees for 15 minutes. Cool in tin and remove gently.

YIELD: 1 DOZEN MUFFINS

Chorizo and Egg Burritos

4 flour tortillas

1 pound chorizo sausage

½ cup chopped onion

4 eggs

½ teaspoon salt

½ teaspoon pepper

2 cups shredded Mexican cheese blend

Salsa and sour cream for garnish

Roll each tortilla in damp paper towel and place in warm (250 degree) oven. Brown sausage and onion together. In separate pan, scramble eggs with salt and pepper. Unroll warm tortillas and fill with sausage, eggs, and cheese. Roll up, place in baking dish, and return to oven for 10 minutes. Serve garnished with salsa and sour cream.

YIELD: 4 SERVINGS

Five Candies a-Boiling

Christmas, my child,
is love in action.
Every time we love,
every time we give,
it's Christmas.

DALE EVANS

How amazing, Father, is the sweet fellowship
we enjoy with You, the God of the universe!
You came to us, became one of us, so that we
live in the peace, assurance, and gladness
of knowing You as our Savior and Lord.
Thank You! Amen.

How sweet your words taste to me;
they are sweeter than honey.

PSALM 119:103 NLT

Pecan Pralines

3 cups sugar

1 cup milk

2 tablespoons light corn syrup

1 teaspoon salt

1 tablespoon butter

1 teaspoon vanilla

3 cups pecan halves

In large saucepan, cook sugar, milk, corn syrup, and salt to soft-ball stage (236 degrees). Remove from heat. Add butter and vanilla, stirring mixture for 2 minutes until slightly opaque. Stir in pecans. Drop immediately onto wax paper and allow to set.

YIELD: 25 PRALINES

No-Fail Fudge

4 cups sugar

1 cup butter

1 teaspoon vanilla

1 cup milk

1 teaspoon salt

1 (6 ounce) package semisweet chocolate chips

1 (6 ounce) package milk chocolate chips

25 large or 4 cups mini marshmallows

1 cup chopped walnuts (optional)

Combine first five ingredients in large saucepan. Bring to soft boil and allow to boil for 2 minutes. Remove from heat and stir in chocolate chips and marshmallows until melted and smooth. Stir in walnuts if desired. Pour into buttered 9x13-inch pan and refrigerate until set.

YIELD: 48 CUBES

Cream Cheese Mints

* * *

2 pounds powdered sugar

1 (8 ounce) package cream cheese, softened

2 drops flavoring (vanilla, peppermint, lemon, cinnamon, etc.)

Food coloring of your choice

Mix all ingredients together. Knead until mixture resembles pie dough. Pinch together small amounts, roll in very fine *sugar*, and press into small molds. Pop out immediately. Store refrigerated in airtight container.

YIELD: 150 MINTS

Reindeer Mix

* * *

1 cup toasted corn squares cereal

1 cup toasted rice squares cereal

1 cup toasted oats cereal

1 cup salted mixed nuts

½ cup butter, melted

1 cup miniature salted pretzels

1 cup Boston Baked Beans candy

1 cup Christmas M&M's

1 cup dried cranberries (such as Craisins)

Combine cereal and nuts and spread in jelly roll pan. Pour butter over all and toss. Bake at 250 degrees for 1 hour. Cool completely and mix with remaining ingredients. Store in airtight container.

YIELD: 8 CUPS

Cornflake Candies

1 cup sugar

1 cup light corn syrup

1 cup peanut butter

½ teaspoon salt

6 cups cornflakes

Combine sugar and corn syrup in heavy saucepan and heat slowly until sugar is dissolved. Stir in peanut butter and salt, then cornflakes. Pour onto wax paper and shape into balls when cool enough to handle.

YIELD: 2 DOZEN CANDIES

Date Roll

3 cups sugar

1 cup whole milk

1 tablespoon butter

½ teaspoon salt

1½ cups pitted and chopped dates

1 teaspoon vanilla

1 cup chopped pecans

½ cup flaked coconut (optional)

In heavy saucepan, combine first four ingredients and cook to soft-ball stage (236 degrees). Add dates and cook gently 3 minutes longer. Remove from heat and stir in vanilla. Cool mixture in pan until lukewarm. Beat until creamy while adding nuts. Turn out onto flat surface and shape into log. Roll in coconut if desired. Cover and chill. Cut into slices before serving.

YIELD: 2 DOZEN SLICES

English Toffee

2 cups sugar

1½ cups butter

2 tablespoons water

½ teaspoon salt

½ cup grated milk chocolate

2 cups chopped pecans

Combine all ingredients (except pecans) and cook over low heat until gently boiling. Cook to hard-ball stage (260 degrees). Spread in jelly roll pan and sprinkle pecans on top. Cool and break into pieces.

YIELD: 1 POUND

Sugared Nuts

3 cups walnut halves

1 cup pecan halves

½ cup whole almonds

2 cups sugar

1 teaspoon salt

1 cup water

½ teaspoon cinnamon

In heavy skillet, combine all ingredients and cook over medium heat, stirring constantly, until water evaporates and nuts take on a sugary appearance. Turn out onto wax paper and separate clumps to cool.

YIELD: 5 CUPS

Apricot Balls

8 ounces dried apricots, finely chopped

2½ cups sweetened flaked coconut

¾ cup sweetened condensed milk

1 cup finely chopped pecans

Mix apricots, coconut, and condensed milk. Chill. Shape into balls and roll in pecans. Store refrigerated in airtight container.

YIELD: 1½ DOZEN BALLS

Gold Nuggets

1 pound powdered sugar

6 tablespoons melted butter

2 tablespoons orange juice

½ teaspoon salt

½ teaspoon vanilla

8 ounces dried pineapple, chopped

1 cup finely chopped cashews

In large bowl, combine powdered sugar, butter, orange juice, salt, and vanilla. Add pineapple and mix well. Chill. Shape into 2-inch balls and roll in nuts. Store refrigerated in airtight container.

YIELD: 3 DOZEN NUGGETS

Peanut Brittle

3 cups sugar

1 cup light corn syrup

½ cup water

3 cups roasted peanuts

1½ tablespoons butter

1 teaspoon baking soda

1 teaspoon vanilla

1 teaspoon salt

Combine sugar, corn syrup, and water in heavy saucepan and cook to soft-ball stage (236 degrees). Add peanuts and butter and continue cooking until mixture takes on a light brown color (290 degrees). Remove from heat and stir in baking soda, vanilla, and salt. Stir until mixture begins to cool and thicken. Pour into buttered jelly roll pan and allow to cool and harden. Break into bite-size pieces.

YIELD: 1½ POUNDS

Divinity Candy

3 cups sugar

1 cup light corn syrup

½ cup water

1 teaspoon salt

3 egg whites, beaten until stiff

1 cup chopped pistachios, toasted

1 teaspoon vanilla

In heavy saucepan, cook first four ingredients to soft-ball stage (236 degrees). Gently pour syrup over egg whites and fold together until creamy. Fold in nuts and vanilla. Drop by tablespoon onto wax paper.

YIELD: 2 DOZEN CANDIES

Sesame Chews

3 cups sesame seeds
1 cup flaked coconut
1 cup honey
1 cup water

1 cup sugar
1 teaspoon salt
2 tablespoons butter

Combine sesame seeds and coconut in large bowl. In heavy saucepan, cook remaining ingredients to hard-ball stage (260 degrees). Pour over seeds and coconut in bowl. Stir until cool enough to handle. Turn out onto buttered surface and shape into thick rope. Cut into bite-size pieces and allow to cool. Store in airtight container.

YIELD: 1½ POUNDS

Homemade Tootsie Rolls

1 tablespoon butter
2 tablespoons light corn syrup
1½ tablespoons cocoa
½ teaspoon salt

¼ teaspoon vanilla
12 tablespoons powdered sugar
3 tablespoons instant dry milk

Combine all ingredients in gallon plastic bag and squeeze together until thoroughly mixed. Chill. Roll on cold surface until long rope is formed. Snip into bite-size pieces.

YIELD: 2 DOZEN

Caramel Corn

2 cups brown sugar

½ cup light corn syrup

2 sticks (1 cup) butter

¼ teaspoon cream of tartar

1 teaspoon salt

1 teaspoon baking soda

6 quarts freshly popped corn

In large saucepan, combine first five ingredients and cook to hard-ball stage (260 degrees). Remove from heat and stir in baking soda thoroughly. Pour mixture over popcorn in large roasting pan and stir until all kernels are coated. Bake at 200 degrees for 1 hour, stirring every 20 minutes. Immediately turn out onto wax paper to cool.

YIELD: 6 QUARTS

Butterscotch Log

1 (6 ounce) package butterscotch
  chips

⅓ cup sweetened condensed milk

½ teaspoon salt

½ teaspoon vanilla

1½ cups finely chopped pecans,
  divided

Melt chips in milk in bowl over pan of simmering water. Stir in salt, vanilla, and half of chopped nuts. Mix well and chill. Turn out onto wax paper and shape into 12-inch log. Roll in remaining pecans and cut into ½-inch slices.

YIELD: 2 DOZEN SLICES

Peanut Butter Kisses

1 cup light corn syrup

1 cup crunchy peanut butter

1½ cups instant dry milk

1 cup powdered sugar

3 cups crisp rice cereal

Combine corn syrup and peanut butter. Add dry milk and powdered sugar. Stir until smooth. Add cereal and shape into 2-inch balls.

YIELD: 2 DOZEN KISSES

Stuffed Dates

3 tablespoons butter, softened

3 tablespoons light corn syrup

1 teaspoon finely grated orange peel

¼ teaspoon salt

½ teaspoon vanilla

2 cups powdered sugar

3 dozen pitted dates

3 dozen whole salted cashews

Cream together butter, corn syrup, orange peel, salt, and vanilla. Add powdered sugar and mix well. Turn out onto wax paper and knead until smooth. Enclose cashews in about 1 teaspoon of mixture and stuff into dates.

YIELD: 3 DOZEN STUFFED DATES

Pecan Turtles

24 soft caramels

2 tablespoons evaporated milk

½ teaspoon salt

16 ounces milk chocolate chips

1½ cups pecan halves

Melt caramels in milk in bowl over pan of simmering water, stirring constantly. Remove from heat and let cool slightly; add salt. Melt chocolate chips. Spoon chocolate like little puddles on wax paper. Before chocolate sets, sink pecan half into edges of chocolate for turtle's head and feet. Spoon thickened caramel mixture into center and cover with more chocolate, leaving turtle's head and feet sticking out slightly.

YIELD: 2 DOZEN TURTLES

Six Cookies a-Cooling

Expectancy is the
atmosphere for miracles.

EDWIN LOUIS COLE

Lord, we long to celebrate Your birth in
myriad ways. Bless us as we feast and rejoice
with full hearts this Christmas season.
Come among us and inspire our worship
as only You can do! Amen.

The house of Israel named it manna,
and it was like coriander seed, white,
and its taste was like wafers with honey.

EXODUS 16:31 NASB

Molasses Hermits

½ cup brown sugar

½ cup shortening

1 tablespoon vinegar

½ cup molasses

½ cup freshly brewed coffee

2½ cups flour

1 teaspoon baking soda

1 teaspoon salt

1 teaspoon ginger

1 dash ground cloves

½ teaspoon cinnamon

Cream together brown sugar and shortening. Add vinegar, molasses, and coffee. In separate bowl, combine dry ingredients and add to creamed mixture. Drop by tablespoon onto greased baking sheet and bake at 350 degrees for about 10 minutes.

YIELD: 3 DOZEN COOKIES

Old-Fashioned Sugar Cookies

* * *

½ cup butter

1 cup sugar

2 eggs

½ teaspoon vanilla

2 cups flour

3 tablespoons baking powder

½ teaspoon salt

Cream together butter, sugar, eggs, and vanilla. In separate bowl, combine dry ingredients and add to creamed mixture. Roll dough very thin, cut into shapes, and arrange on lightly greased baking sheet. Bake at 350 degrees for 12 minutes.

YIELD: 2½ DOZEN COOKIES

Chocolate Candy Cups

1 pound high-quality milk chocolate

1 pound high-quality dark chocolate

1 pound high-quality white chocolate

Nuts, dried fruit, or crushed peppermint candy for garnish

Break up chocolate and place each kind separately in deep bowls or glass measuring cups with pouring spouts. Set down in gently simmering shallow pan of water. Allow chocolate to melt slowly, stirring occasionally. When melted, pour into paper-lined mini muffin tins until half full. Place nut, piece of dried fruit, or crushed candy atop each and allow to harden.

YIELD: 3 POUNDS

Haystacks

1½ cups semisweet chocolate chips

½ cup peanut butter

¼ teaspoon salt

2½ cups chow mein noodles

½ cup peanuts

Melt chocolate in bowl over pan of simmering water until melted. Stir in peanut butter and salt. Remove from heat; add noodles and peanuts. Drop by tablespoon onto wax paper and let harden.

YIELD: 2 DOZEN HAYSTACKS

Christmas M&M Cookies

* * *

1 cup shortening

½ cup sugar

1 cup brown sugar

2 eggs

2 teaspoons vanilla

2¼ cups flour

1 teaspoon baking soda

½ teaspoon salt

2 cups Christmas M&M's

Cream together shortening, sugars, eggs, and vanilla. In separate bowl, combine flour, baking soda, and salt. Add to creamed mixture and gently stir in M&M's. Bake at 350 degrees for 10 to 12 minutes.

YIELD: 3 DOZEN COOKIES

Seven-Layer Cookies

* * *

½ cup butter

2 dashes salt

1 cup graham cracker crumbs

1 cup milk chocolate chips

1 cup butterscotch chips

1 cup semisweet chocolate chips

1 cup flaked coconut

1 cup chopped pecans

1 (14 ounce) can sweetened condensed milk

Melt butter and salt in 8x11-inch pan. Stir in graham cracker crumbs and pat down evenly to form crust. On top of crust, layer remaining ingredients (except milk) in order given. Drizzle milk over top. Bake at 350 degrees for 25 to 30 minutes. Allow to cool before cutting into bars.

YIELD: 2 DOZEN COOKIES

Gingerbread Men

1 cup brown sugar

⅓ cup shortening

1½ cups molasses

⅔ cup water

7 cups flour

2 teaspoons baking soda

2 teaspoons ginger

1 teaspoon salt

1 teaspoon allspice

1 teaspoon ground cloves

1 teaspoon cinnamon

In large bowl, cream together brown sugar, shortening, molasses, and water. In separate bowl, combine dry ingredients and add to creamed mixture. Refrigerate for 2 hours. Roll out one-third of dough at a time. Cut with gingerbread man cutter and place on lightly greased baking sheet. Bake at 350 degrees for 10 to 12 minutes. When cool, frost and decorate as desired.

YIELD: 2 DOZEN GINGERBREAD MEN

Pecan Tessies

6 ounces cream cheese, softened

1 cup butter, softened

2 cups flour

½ teaspoon salt

FILLING:

2 eggs

1½ cups brown sugar

2 tablespoons butter

2 teaspoons vanilla

1½ cups chopped pecans

Blend cream cheese and butter. Stir in flour and salt and refrigerate for 1 hour. Press into ungreased mini muffin tins and set aside. Cream together eggs, brown sugar, butter, and vanilla. Add pecans and mix well. Pour filling over dough in muffin tins and bake at 325 degrees for about 20 minutes.

YIELD: 2 DOZEN TESSIES

Maple Rollouts

¼ cup shortening

¼ cup butter

1 cup sugar

1 cup maple syrup

1 cup sour cream

2 eggs, beaten

1 teaspoon vanilla

3 cups flour

1 teaspoon baking soda

1 teaspoon salt

Cream together shortening, butter, and sugar. Add maple syrup and sour cream. Blend together eggs and vanilla and stir into creamed mixture alternately with combined dry ingredients. Don't overwork dough. Refrigerate for 2 hours. Roll out and cut with leaf-shaped cookie cutter. Place on lightly greased baking sheet. Bake at 350 degrees for 8 to 10 minutes.

YIELD: 4 DOZEN ROLLOUTS

Coconut Macaroons

2 egg whites

¼ teaspoon salt

¼ teaspoon vanilla

⅔ cup sugar

1¼ cups flaked coconut

Beat eggs whites, salt, and vanilla until soft peaks form. Add sugar a little at a time, beating until stiff. Fold in coconut and drop by tablespoon onto lightly greased baking sheet. Bake at 325 degrees for 20 minutes.

YIELD: 1½ DOZEN MACAROONS

Festive Peanut Butter Cookies

½ cup butter, softened

½ cup crunchy peanut butter

½ cup sugar

½ cup brown sugar

1 egg, beaten

1 teaspoon vanilla

1 teaspoon salt

½ teaspoon baking soda

1¼ cups flour

Red and green decorating sugars

Cream together butter, peanut butter, sugars, egg, and vanilla. In separate bowl, combine dry ingredients and add to creamed mixture. Roll dough into 2-inch balls and place on ungreased baking sheet. Lightly flatten each with crisscross of fork tines. Sprinkle lightly with decorating sugars and bake at 350 degrees for 10 minutes. Do not overbake!

YIELD: 2 DOZEN COOKIES

Snickerdoodles

½ cup butter

½ cup shortening

2 eggs

2½ cups flour

2 teaspoons cream of tartar

1 teaspoon baking soda

½ teaspoon salt

2 tablespoons sugar

2 teaspoons cinnamon

Cream together butter, shortening, and eggs. In separate bowl, combine flour, cream of tartar, soda, and salt. Add to creamed mixture. In small bowl, combine sugar and cinnamon. Roll walnut-size balls of dough in sugar mixture and place on ungreased baking sheet. Bake at 350 degrees for 8 to 10 minutes.

YIELD: 3 DOZEN COOKIES

Thumbprint Cookies

½ cup butter

½ cup shortening

2 eggs

2 cups flour

½ teaspoon salt

¼ teaspoon baking soda

1 teaspoon vanilla

Favorite jam or preserves

Cream together butter, shortening, and eggs. In separate bowl, combine dry ingredients and add to creamed mixture. Stir in vanilla. Roll dough into 2-inch balls and place on ungreased baking sheet. Bake at 350 degrees for 5 minutes. Remove from oven and gently indent each cookie with your thumb or bowl of small spoon. Add jam and bake 5 minutes longer.

YIELD: 2 DOZEN COOKIES

Applesauce Cookies

½ cup shortening

1 cup sugar

1 cup unsweetened applesauce

2 cups flour

1 teaspoon baking soda

½ teaspoon salt

1 teaspoon cinnamon

½ teaspoon ground cloves

½ cup chopped raisins

½ cup chopped nuts

Cream together shortening, sugar, and applesauce. In separate bowl, combine flour, baking soda, salt, and spices. Add to creamed mixture. Stir in raisins and nuts. Drop by tablespoon onto greased baking sheet and bake at 350 degrees for 12 minutes.

Yield: 4 dozen cookies

Buckeyes

3 pounds powdered sugar

2 cups butter, softened

2½ cups peanut butter, smooth or crunchy (avoid natural or reduced fat)

1 teaspoon salt

2 (12 ounce) packages semisweet or milk chocolate chips

Cream together powdered sugar, butter, peanut butter, and salt. Shape into walnut-size balls and place on wax paper–lined baking sheet. Refrigerate for 2 hours. Melt chocolate chips in bowl over pan of simmering water. Using toothpick, dip each ball into chocolate to coat. Place back onto wax paper and refrigerate until set.

Yield: 8 dozen buckeyes

Mexican Holiday Cookies

2 cups butter

1 cup sugar

1 egg

1 teaspoon vanilla

5 cups flour

1 teaspoon baking soda

½ teaspoon ground cloves

1 teaspoon cinnamon

½ teaspoon ground anise

1 teaspoon salt

Juice of 1 orange (about ¼ cup)

Cinnamon and sugar for dusting

Cream together butter, sugar, egg, and vanilla. In separate bowl, combine dry ingredients and add to creamed mixture. Stir in orange juice. Roll out on floured surface and cut into desired shapes. Place on ungreased baking sheet and bake at 350 degrees for 8 minutes. Cool just until firm, then dust with cinnamon-sugar mixture.

YIELD: 3 DOZEN COOKIES

Orange-Iced Cranberry Cookies

································ ⭐ ································ ⭐ ································ ⭐ ································

½ cup butter, softened

½ cup sugar

½ cup brown sugar

½ cup sour cream

1 teaspoon vanilla

2 eggs, beaten

2¼ cups flour

½ teaspoon baking soda

½ teaspoon baking powder

½ teaspoon salt

½ cup dried cranberries (such as Craisins), chopped

¼ cup orange juice

1 can buttercream frosting

Cream together butter, sugars, sour cream, vanilla, and eggs. In separate bowl, combine flour, baking soda, baking powder, and salt. Add to creamed mixture. Stir in dried cranberries. Drop by tablespoon onto lightly greased baking sheet and bake at 350 degrees for 12 minutes. When cool, add orange juice to buttercream frosting and ice cookies.

YIELD: 2½ DOZEN COOKIES

Rosemary Crescents

½ cup shortening

1 cup sugar

1 egg

5 cups flour

1 teaspoon baking powder

1 teaspoon baking soda

½ teaspoon salt

1 teaspoon dried rosemary, finely ground

1 cup buttermilk

Powdered sugar for dusting

Cream together shortening, sugar, and egg. In separate bowl, combine flour, baking powder, baking soda, salt, and rosemary. Add to creamed mixture alternately with buttermilk. Cover and refrigerate for 2 hours. Roll out to ½-inch thickness and cut into 3-inch circles with cookie cutter. Halve each circle and gently shape halves into crescents. Place on greased baking sheet and bake at 350 degrees for 10 minutes. While cookies are still slightly warm, dust lightly with powdered sugar.

YIELD: 6 DOZEN CRESCENTS

Date-Filled Cookies

1 cup shortening

2 cups brown sugar

3 eggs, beaten

½ cup water

1 teaspoon vanilla

3½ cups flour

½ teaspoon salt

1 teaspoon baking soda

2 dashes cinnamon

FILLING:

2 cups chopped dates

¾ cup sugar

¾ cup water

½ cup chopped nuts

Cream together shortening, brown sugar, eggs, water, and vanilla. In separate bowl, combine dry ingredients and add to creamed mixture. Drop by tablespoon onto lightly greased baking sheet. For filling, combine dates, sugar, and water in saucepan. Cook until thickened. Add nuts. Put about ½ teaspoon date filling in center of each cookie. Top with ½ teaspoon dough. Bake at 375 degrees for 10 to 12 minutes.

YIELD: 6 DOZEN COOKIES

Scottish Shortbread

1 cup shortening

½ cup sugar

½ cup brown sugar

3 egg yolks

¼ cup whole milk

2 teaspoons vanilla

2½ cups flour

2 teaspoons cream of tartar

1 teaspoon baking soda

½ teaspoon salt

Cream together shortening, sugars, and egg yolks. Add milk and vanilla. In separate bowl, combine dry ingredients and add to creamed mixture. Refrigerate for 1 hour. Roll out to ½-inch thickness and cut into 2-inch squares. Place on ungreased baking sheet and bake at 350 degrees for 10 to 12 minutes.

Yield: 2 dozen cookies

Seven Desserts a-Delighting

I will honor Christmas in my heart
and try to keep it all the year.

CHARLES DICKENS

Jesus, life with You is sweeter each day!
Open our arms and hearts to include the
lonely and forgotten ones all around us,
and fill every soul to the brim with the gifts
of Your warm, welcoming grace. Amen.

*I will be fully satisfied as with the
richest of foods; with singing lips
my mouth will praise you.*

Psalm 63:5 NIV

Swedish Cream

1½ envelopes unflavored gelatin

2 tablespoons warm water

1 pint whipping cream

1 cup sugar

1 teaspoon salt

1 pint sour cream

1 teaspoon vanilla

In heavy saucepan, soak gelatin in warm water for 10 minutes. Add whipping cream, sugar, and salt. Cook on low until gelatin is dissolved, stirring constantly. Remove from heat and stir in sour cream and vanilla. Pour into individual serving molds or one large mold. Refrigerate for several hours or overnight until cold and well set. Serve with sweetened fresh or frozen fruit.

YIELD: 12 SERVINGS

Quick and Easy Lemon Cake

CAKE:

1 box yellow cake mix

1 (3 ounce) package lemon gelatin

¾ cup vegetable oil

¾ cup water

4 eggs

½ teaspoon salt

GLAZE:

2 tablespoons butter

⅓ cup lemon juice

2 cups powdered sugar

Beat all cake ingredients together and pour into greased 9x13-inch pan. Bake at 350 degrees for 40 minutes. Remove from oven and immediately prick holes all over top with toothpick. Allow to cool. For glaze, combine all glaze ingredients in saucepan and bring to boil. Pour hot glaze over cooled cake.

Oatmeal Cake

1 ¾ cups boiling water

1 cup rolled oats

1 cup sugar

1 cup brown sugar

½ cup butter

2 eggs

1 ¾ cups flour

1 teaspoon salt

1 teaspoon baking soda

1 tablespoon cocoa

1 (12 ounce) package chocolate chips, divided

¾ cup chopped nuts

Pour boiling water over oats and let stand for 10 minutes. Stir in sugars, butter, and eggs. In separate bowl, combine flour, salt, baking soda, and cocoa and add to oat mixture. Blend well. Add half of chocolate chips. Pour into greased and floured 9x13-inch pan. Sprinkle with remaining chocolate chips and nuts. Bake at 350 degrees for 35 to 40 minutes.

Raspberries in Vanilla Sauce

* * *

Raspberries, washed and drained dry

1 cup heavy cream

1 cup half-and-half

⅓ cup sugar

4 egg yolks

½ teaspoon salt

1 teaspoon vanilla

Place berries in individual serving bowls (martini glasses make an elegant presentation). In heavy saucepan, gently whisk together remaining ingredients (except vanilla) and cook over medium heat until thickened, but do not allow to boil. Stir in vanilla. Cool completely and refrigerate. When ready to serve, whisk gently for a few seconds and pour over raspberries. (Any type of fresh berries may be substituted for the raspberries.)

YIELD: 4–6 SERVINGS

Angel Delight

* * *

1 angel food cake

1 pint whipping cream

1 package sweetened frozen fruit, thawed

Break up cake into large chunks. Whip cream. Fold fruit and cake pieces into cream. Spoon into serving bowl and refrigerate for 2 to 3 hours.

YIELD: 10–12 SERVINGS

Cranberry Paradise Bars

2½ cups flour

2½ teaspoons baking powder

½ teaspoon salt

¼ cup butter, softened

¼ cup shortening

1¾ cups brown sugar

3 eggs

1 teaspoon vanilla

½ teaspoon orange extract

½ cup white chocolate chips

½ cup orange-flavored dried cranberries (such as Craisins)

Combine flour, baking powder, and salt. In separate bowl, cream together butter, shortening, brown sugar, eggs, vanilla, and orange extract. Stir in flour mixture, ½ cup at a time. Stir in white chocolate chips and cranberries. Spread in greased jelly roll pan and bake at 350 degrees for 20 minutes. When cool, cut into bars.

YIELD: 1 DOZEN BARS

Pear Betty

4–5 ripe pears

1½ teaspoons lemon juice

2 tablespoons cornstarch

2 teaspoons cinnamon

¼ cup sugar

¼ cup brown sugar

½ teaspoon salt

TOPPING:

½ cup quick-cooking oats

½ cup brown sugar

3 tablespoons flour

1 teaspoon cinnamon

½ teaspoon nutmeg

1 dash salt

¼ cup chopped pecans

⅔ cup butter, melted

Peel, core, and slice pears. Gently combine with next six ingredients. Pour into greased 8x11-inch baking dish. Stir together topping ingredients and spread mixture over pears. Bake at 350 degrees for 30 to 40 minutes.

YIELD: 8 SERVINGS

Pumpkin Roll

1 cup sugar

3 eggs

¾ cup flour

⅔ cup canned prepared pumpkin

2 teaspoons cinnamon

1 teaspoon baking soda

½ teaspoon salt

½ cup powdered sugar

FILLING:

1 (8 ounce) package cream cheese, softened

¼ cup butter, softened

1 cup powdered sugar

1 teaspoon vanilla

¼ teaspoon salt

Cream together sugar and eggs. Add in next six ingredients and mix well. Lightly grease jelly roll pan and line with wax paper. Pour batter into pan and bake at 375 degrees for 15 minutes. Cool in pan for 5 minutes. Flip out onto tea towel covered with powdered sugar. Peel off wax paper. Gently roll up cake and let stand for 30 minutes. For filling, cream together cream cheese, butter, and powdered sugar. Add vanilla and salt. Blend well. Unroll cake and spread with filling. Gently roll up again and refrigerate for 2 hours. Slice into pinwheels.

YIELD: 10–12 SLICES

Fruity Cranberry Crisp

1½ cups fresh cranberries, cooked

½ cup dried cherries, chopped

1 teaspoon lemon juice

⅔ cup real maple syrup

2 Granny Smith apples, peeled, cored, and cubed

2 pears, peeled, cored, and cubed

¼ cup flour

TOPPING:

1 cup quick-cooking oats

¼ teaspoon each cinnamon, nutmeg, ground cloves, and ginger

1 teaspoon salt

¼ cup brown sugar

¼ cup chopped walnuts

Drain excess liquid from cranberries and combine with cherries. Add lemon juice and maple syrup and stir lightly. Toss apples and pears in flour. Arrange in buttered 8x11-inch baking dish and pour berry mixture over all. Combine all topping ingredients and spread over fruit. Dot liberally with *butter* and bake at 350 degrees for 35 to 40 minutes.

YIELD: 8–10 SERVINGS

Pumpkin Pie

1 (15 ounce) can prepared pumpkin

⅔ cup sugar

½ teaspoon salt

1 teaspoon cinnamon

½ teaspoon ginger

½ teaspoon ground cloves

3 eggs, beaten

1 (12 ounce) can evaporated milk

1 pastry shell, unbaked

Combine pumpkin, sugar, salt, and spices. Whisk in eggs and evaporated milk. Pour into pastry shell and bake at 400 degrees for 15 minutes. Reduce oven temperature to 325 degrees and continue baking for 45 minutes.

YIELD: 8 SLICES

Caramel Nut Pudding

¾ cup brown sugar

1 cup water

1 tablespoon butter, melted

1 cup flour

2 teaspoons baking powder

½ teaspoon salt

½ cup chopped nuts

¼ cup brown sugar

⅓ cup whole milk

Whipped cream for garnish

Combine ¾ cup brown sugar, water, and butter and set aside. In large bowl, mix together flour, baking powder, salt, nuts, ¼ cup brown sugar, and milk. Spread in greased 9-inch square pan. Pour sugar mixture over top and bake at 375 degrees for 30 minutes. Serve with whipped cream.

YIELD: 6–8 SERVINGS

Cayman Islands Peach Cobbler

4 tablespoons butter

1 cup sugar

¾ cup whole milk

1 cup flour

1 teaspoon baking powder

½ teaspoon salt

2 cups fresh or frozen sliced peaches

Melt butter and pour into four or six large ramekins. Blend together sugar, milk, flour, baking powder, and salt. Divide batter among ramekins, spooning it over butter, but do not stir. Place peaches on top of batter and bake at 350 degrees for 40 minutes. Serve warm with scoop of vanilla ice cream.

YEILD: 4–6 SERVINGS

Rice Pudding

3 cups whole milk

1½ cups instant rice

½ teaspoon salt

½ teaspoon cinnamon

¼ teaspoon nutmeg

3 tablespoons butter

3 tablespoons sugar

2 eggs, beaten

1 teaspoon vanilla

Raisins (optional)

Heat milk to nearly boiling; add rice, salt, spices, and butter. Reduce heat, cover, and simmer slowly for about 10 minutes, stirring once. Stir in sugar and eggs and simmer 1 minute longer. Remove from heat and add vanilla. Cool. Add raisins if desired. Cover and store in refrigerator.

YIELD: 8 SERVINGS

Baked Bananas Deluxe

• • • • • • ✦ • • • • • • • • • • • ✦ • • • • • • • • • • • ✦ • • • • • • • •

6 bananas

1 tablespoon lemon juice

2 dashes salt

3 tablespoons brown sugar

1 cup maraschino cherries, with syrup

Peel bananas and cut in half lengthwise. Arrange in greased shallow baking dish. Sprinkle with lemon juice, salt, and brown sugar. Drain cherries (reserving syrup) and spread over banana mixture. Brush with reserved syrup and bake at 400 degrees for about 30 minutes or until bananas are soft. Generously baste with syrup twice more during baking. Serve over ice cream.

YIELD: 6 SERVINGS

Peanut Butter Pie

• • • • • • ✦ • • • • • • • • • • • ✦ • • • • • • • • • • • ✦ • • • • • • • •

1 (8 ounce) package cream cheese, softened

1 cup crunchy peanut butter

½ teaspoon salt

1 (16 ounce) tub frozen whipped topping, thawed

1½ cups powdered sugar

2 (9 inch) graham cracker crusts

In large mixing bowl, beat together cream cheese, peanut butter, and salt until light and fluffy. Gradually whisk in whipped topping and powdered sugar until smooth. Pour into crusts and refrigerate for 8 hours.

YIELD: 2 PIES

122

Philly Pound Cake

2 cups flour
1½ tablespoons baking powder
1 teaspoon salt
1 (8 ounce) package cream cheese, softened

¾ cup butter, softened
1½ cups sugar
1½ teaspoons vanilla
4 eggs
Powdered sugar for dusting

In small bowl, stir together flour, baking powder, and salt. Set aside. Combine cream cheese, butter, sugar, and vanilla with mixer on low speed. Add flour mixture and eggs alternately. Pour into well-greased loaf pan and bake at 325 degrees for 1 hour and 20 minutes. Cool in pan before removing and dusting with powdered sugar.

YIELD: 12 SERVINGS

Chocolate Pots de Crème

1½ cups half-and-half

6 tablespoons sugar

½ cup semisweet chocolate chips

4 egg yolks

½ teaspoon salt

1 teaspoon vanilla

Whipped cream and chocolate
shavings for garnish

Place four small ramekins or custard dishes in shallow baking dish. In medium saucepan, heat half-and-half and sugar to steaming, but not boiling. Remove from heat and whisk in chocolate chips until melted. Stir in egg yolks, salt, and vanilla and pour into ramekins. Pour boiling *water* into baking dish halfway up sides of ramekins. Bake at 350 degrees for 20 minutes or until mixture is set (jiggly in center). Cool and serve with whipped cream and chocolate shavings.

YIELD: 4 SERVINGS

Scalloped Apples

5–6 Granny Smith apples, peeled, cored, and sliced

1 teaspoon lemon juice

¾ cup brown sugar

4 tablespoons butter

2 eggs, beaten

½ teaspoon cinnamon

½ teaspoon nutmeg

½ teaspoon salt

2 cups crushed butter-flavored crackers

In large saucepan, cook apples for about 15 minutes, until slightly softened. Stir in lemon juice, brown sugar, butter, eggs, and spices. Grease 9x11-inch baking dish and cover bottom with layer of cracker crumbs, followed by layer of apple mixture. Continue alternating layers, ending with crumbs on top. Bake at 350 degrees for 45 minutes.

YIELD: 6 SERVINGS

Easy Crème Brûlée

2 cups heavy whipping cream

4 egg yolks, beaten

3 tablespoons sugar

¼ teaspoon salt

1 teaspoon vanilla

Fine brown sugar for glaze

In heavy saucepan, combine cream, egg yolks, sugar, and salt. Cook over low heat, stirring constantly, until mixture thickens. Remove from heat and stir in vanilla. Pour into four ramekins or custard dishes and refrigerate for several hours. When ready to serve, top with light layer of brown sugar and place under broiler just until sugar liquefies. Watch carefully to avoid burning. Remove from broiler and allow sugar to reharden as it cools.

YIELD: 4 SERVINGS

Eight Kids a-Cooking

Christmas makes me
happy no matter what time
of year it comes around.

BRYAN WHITE

Lord, remind us often that love is the most important ingredient in acts of hospitality. As we welcome others into our homes and lives, through all our efforts to care and comfort and nourish, let Your love flowing through us be the main course! Amen.

Oh, taste and see that the Lord is good;
blessed is the man who trusts in Him!

Psalm 34:8 nkjv

Macaroni and Cheese

2 cups uncooked macaroni

1 teaspoon salt

½ teaspoon pepper

3 tablespoons butter, melted

1 tablespoon flour

1½ cups milk

1 cup shredded cheddar cheese

1 cup shredded pasteurized process
   cheese spread

½ cup bread crumbs

Cook macaroni according to package directions. Drain. Place half of macaroni in bottom of baking dish. In skillet, whisk together salt, pepper, butter, flour, and milk; simmer to make white sauce. Stir cheeses into sauce until melted and pour half over macaroni. Repeat macaroni and sauce layers. Top with bread crumbs and bake at 375 degrees for 30 minutes.

YIELD: 6 SERVINGS

Eggs in Ham Nests

2 tablespoons butter, melted

2 tablespoons flour

½ teaspoon salt

¼ teaspoon pepper

¼ teaspoon dry mustard

1 cup whole milk

1¾ cups finely chopped cooked ham

6 eggs

Paprika

In skillet, whisk together butter, flour, salt, pepper, and dry mustard, creating a paste. Whisk in milk and cook slowly until thickened. Stir in ham. Press into six lightly greased muffin cups and crack 1 egg into each. Sprinkle lightly with paprika and bake at 325 degrees for 25 minutes. Cool slightly and use fork to gently lift out onto plates.

YIELD: 6 NESTS

Fruit Smoothies

1 cup strawberry yogurt

½ cup blueberries

½ cup strawberries or peaches

2 tablespoons protein powder

¾ cup whole milk

1 tablespoon honey

1 dash salt

½ cup crushed ice

Combine all ingredients in blender and blend until smooth.

YIELD: 3–4 SMALL SERVINGS

Chicken Noodle Soup

1 chicken breast, cooked and
  chopped

1 quart chicken broth

¼ teaspoon salt

¼ teaspoon pepper

1 teaspoon dried minced onion

½ teaspoon parsley flakes

1 dash paprika

½ cup cubed carrots

¼ cup thinly sliced celery

1 cup uncooked thin egg noodles

In large Dutch oven, combine all ingredients (except noodles) and simmer for 25 minutes or until vegetables are soft. Add noodles and cook 10 minutes longer or until noodles are soft.

YIELD: 6 SERVINGS

Spaghetti and Meatballs

½ pound lean ground beef

½ pound Italian sausage

1 cup shredded white bread

1 egg, beaten

1 generous dash each salt, pepper, and celery salt

2 tablespoons milk

7 ounces uncooked spaghetti noodles

1 jar spaghetti sauce

Grated Parmesan cheese

Blend first six ingredients well, using hands to mix. Shape into 2-inch meatballs and brown well in hot *oil*. Drain on paper towels. Prepare spaghetti according to package directions. Drain and pour into large serving dish. Top with meatballs and pour spaghetti sauce over all. Sprinkle with cheese.

YIELD: 6 SERVINGS

Chunky Applesauce

12 Granny Smith apples, peeled, cored, and quartered

2 cups water

1 teaspoon salt

1 cup sugar

½ cup brown sugar

1 teaspoon cinnamon

In large kettle, simmer apples in water and salt until very tender, almost mushy, stirring often. Add sugars and cinnamon. Using potato masher, work apples into chunky pulp.

YIELD: 8 CUPS

Chocolate Chip Pancakes

1 cup flour

¼ teaspoon salt

2 teaspoons baking powder

1 egg, beaten

¼ cup vegetable oil

⅔ cup whole milk

Chocolate chips

Combine all ingredients (except chocolate chips and maple syrup) in mixing bowl with spout for pouring. Use more or less milk to make thick but pourable batter. Pour 3-inch pancakes onto buttered, hot griddle. Immediately dot with chocolate chips. Flip when air bubbles form on surface. Cook 20 to 30 seconds longer. Serve with maple syrup.

YIELD: 1 DOZEN PANCAKES

Sweet Pickles

1 (48 ounce) jar whole dill pickles

1 small onion, sliced

¾ cup white vinegar

2 cups sugar

1 teaspoon pickling spice

Drain pickles and refill jar with very cold *water*. Let pickles soak for 20 minutes. Drain and slice pickles into 1-inch chunks and return to jar. Place onion slices on top of pickles and set aside. In small saucepan, bring vinegar, sugar, and pickling spice to rolling boil. Pour over pickles and screw on jar lid. Let cool on counter for 30 minutes. Refrigerate. Pickles will be ready in 24 hours.

YIELD: 1 JAR PICKLES

Oven-Fried Drumsticks

8 chicken legs

⅓ cup shortening

1 cup buttermilk

¼ cup flour

½ teaspoon salt

¼ teaspoon pepper

½ teaspoon paprika

Wash chicken and pat dry with paper towel. Melt shortening and set aside. Pour buttermilk into large bowl and soak chicken legs in it while preparing coating. Mix flour, salt, pepper, and paprika in paper bag. Shake excess buttermilk off two legs at a time and toss chicken in bag to coat well. Arrange chicken in single layer in ungreased shallow baking dish. Drizzle melted shortening over chicken and bake uncovered at 425 degrees for about 45 minutes.

YIELD: 8 SERVINGS

Sloppy Joes

2 pounds ground beef

1 onion, chopped

1 teaspoon salt

½ teaspoon pepper

1 tablespoon Worcestershire sauce

1 cup brown sugar

2½ cups ketchup

½ cup water

1 tablespoon mustard

Brown beef and onion with salt and pepper. Drain off fat and add Worcestershire sauce, brown sugar, ketchup, water, and mustard, mixing well. Cover and simmer for 15 minutes. Serve over hamburger buns.

YIELD: 8–10 SLOPPY JOES

Green Eggs and Ham

1 (½ pound) ham steak

4 eggs

1 drop green food coloring

Salt and pepper to taste

Butter

Slice ham into serving-size pieces and brown in small amount of butter. Beat eggs and stir in food coloring and seasonings. Cook in small amount of butter and serve atop ham.

YIELD: 4 SERVINGS

Frog-Eye Fruit Salad

1 pound uncooked acini di pepe pasta

1 (20 ounce) can crushed pineapple, with juice

1 (15 ounce) can mandarin oranges, with juice

1 cup sugar

½ teaspoon salt

2 tablespoons flour

3 egg yolks, beaten

4 cups mini marshmallows

1 (8 ounce) tub frozen whipped topping, thawed

Cook pasta according to package directions. Drain and set aside. Strain juices off fruit into small saucepan and refrigerate fruit. Mix sugar, salt, and flour and add to pan of juice. Cook until thickened, stirring constantly. Remove from heat. Let cool for 5 minutes; then stir in egg yolks. Return to burner and cook 1 minute longer. Pour over cooled pasta. Cover and refrigerate overnight. Add fruit, marshmallows, and whipped topping and stir well. Chill until ready to serve.

YIELD: 6 CUPS

Apple Butter

1 quart apple cider

6 large apples

½ cup sugar

½ cup brown sugar

1 cup light corn syrup

½ teaspoon salt

½ teaspoon cinnamon

Boil cider until reduced by half. Peel, core, and slice apples. Simmer in cider until mixture begins to thicken. Stir and mash apples to form a pulp as they cook. Add sugars, corn syrup, salt, and cinnamon. Continue to simmer until mixture is spreadable consistency. Store in refrigerator.

YIELD: 3 PINTS

Breakfast Pizza

1 tube refrigerated crescent rolls

½ pound bacon, fried crisp

4 eggs

2 tablespoons cream

Salsa

Salt and pepper to taste

1 cup shredded mozzarella

Gently roll out crescent roll dough into one big rectangle. Transfer to greased 9x11-inch pan. Push edges gently up sides to form a slight ridge. Crumble bacon and spread over dough. Beat eggs with cream and spread over bacon. Top with salsa, salt, pepper, and mozzarella. Bake at 450 degrees for 12 to 15 minutes, just until cheese is melted.

YIELD: 8–10 SLICES

Lemon Drop Cookies

1 cup shortening

2 cups sugar

3 eggs

½ teaspoon lemon extract

1 teaspoon salt

6 tablespoons whole milk

3 cups flour

1 tablespoon baking powder

Crushed lemon drops for garnish

Cream together first six ingredients. Stir in flour and baking powder. Drop by tablespoon onto ungreased baking sheet. Garnish with a few flakes of crushed candy and bake at 350 degrees for 12 minutes.

YIELD: 3 DOZEN COOKIES

Rock Candy

2 cups sugar

½ cup light corn syrup

½ cup water

½ teaspoon flavored oil (lemon, cinnamon, peppermint, etc.)

Food coloring

1 cup powdered sugar

Using candy thermometer, cook sugar, corn syrup, and water to hard-crack stage (300 degrees). Remove from heat and add oil and food coloring. Pour quickly onto greased baking sheet. When mixture cools, it will be one hard slab of candy. Press hard object into center of candy to fracture it into bite-size pieces. Place a few shards at a time in bag of powdered sugar and shake. Transfer to colander and shake to remove all but light sugar dusting.

YIELD: 1½ POUNDS

Green Bean and Corn Casserole

2 (15.5 ounce) cans french-cut green beans, drained

1 (15.5 ounce) can white shoepeg corn, drained

1 (10.5 ounce) can cream of mushroom soup

1 (8 ounce) carton sour cream

½ cup water

1 tablespoon dried minced onion

Salt and pepper to taste

1 sleeve butter-flavored crackers, crushed

½ cup butter, melted

Combine beans, corn, soup, sour cream, water, onion, salt, and pepper in baking dish. Sprinkle crackers on top and drizzle butter over all. Bake at 350 degrees for 30 minutes or until bubbly.

YIELD: 6–8 SERVINGS

No-Bake Krispy Krunch Bars

2 cups peanut butter

2 cups buttercream frosting

2½ cups crisp rice cereal

4 tablespoons butter softened

½ cup peanuts

1 cup semisweet chocolate chips

1 tablespoon butter

Mix together first five ingredients and press into 9x13-inch pan. In saucepan, melt together chocolate chips and 1 tablespoon butter. Drizzle over crunch mixture in baking pan and refrigerate for 1 hour.

Yield: 24 bars

Trail Mix

1 cup salted peanuts

1 cup salted almonds

1 cup M&M's candy

1 cup mixed dried fruit

½ cup butterscotch chips

½ cup milk chocolate chips

1 cup snipped red licorice

2 cups freshly popped corn, lightly buttered and salted

In large mixing bowl, combine first seven ingredients and mix well. Fold in popcorn and enjoy!

YIELD: 8 CUPS

Christmas Kisses

1½ cups flour

1 teaspoon baking soda

½ teaspoon salt

½ cup shortening

1 egg, beaten

2 tablespoons whole milk

½ cup brown sugar

1 teaspoon vanilla

½ cup granulated sugar

1 (12 ounce) bag chocolate kisses

Combine all ingredients except granulated sugar and chocolate kisses.
Shape dough into small balls and roll in sugar. Place on lightly greased
baking sheet and bake at 350 degrees for 8 to 10 minutes. Remove from
oven and immediately press chocolate kiss in center of each cookie. Allow
to cool on baking sheet.

YIELD: 2 DOZEN KISSES

Nine Main Dishes a-Mixing

Christmas means fellowship,
feasting, giving and receiving,
a time of good cheer, home.

W. J. TUCKER

Lord, our souls are hungry for You. Feed us on Your
wonderful Word and help us sense your presence in
all the circumstances of life. Grow us through joy
as well as adversity to realize You are ever
in control, always with us. Amen.

The Lord of Heaven's Armies will spread
a wonderful feast for all the people of the world.
It will be a delicious banquet with clear,
well-aged wine and choice meat.

ISAIAH 25:6 NLT

Foolproof (No Kidding!) Prime Rib

1. Choose a roast that is 5 pounds or larger.
2. Season or rub meat as you prefer, and use an open roasting pan.
3. Preheat oven to 375 degrees.
4. Roast prime rib for 1 hour.
5. Turn off oven but do not open oven door!
6. After 2 hours, turn oven back on to 375 degrees, but remember. . . do not open oven door through entire process!

   Cooking time:
   Rare: 25 minutes
   Medium rare: 35 minutes
   Well done: 45 minutes

7. Cut strings and meat should fall right off the bones. Let meat rest, covered, for 5 minutes. Voila! Perfect prime rib!

YIELD: 6 SERVINGS

Chicken Divan

6 boneless, skinless chicken breasts

1 (16 ounce) bag frozen broccoli florets, thawed

1 cup real mayonnaise

½ teaspoon curry powder

1 teaspoon salt

½ teaspoon pepper

1 teaspoon lemon juice

1 cup shredded sharp cheddar cheese

¼ cup butter, melted

½ cup crushed saltine crackers

Cook chicken breasts in boiling water until just barely cooked through. Remove and drain. Cover bottom of large casserole dish with broccoli. Place chicken atop broccoli. Combine mayo, curry, salt, pepper, lemon juice, and cheese in large mixing bowl. Cover chicken with sauce, drizzle butter over all, and top with crackers. Bake at 350 degrees for 1 hour. Serve over rice.

YIELD: 8 SERVINGS

Marinated Flank Steak

3 pounds flank steak

¾ cup soy sauce

¼ cup vegetable oil

3 tablespoons vinegar

2 tablespoons honey

1½ teaspoons garlic powder

1½ teaspoons ginger

3 green onions, finely snipped

½ teaspoon meat tenderizer

Combine all ingredients in ziplock bag. Refrigerate for up to two days. Grill on high heat for 10 minutes on each side, basting with marinade as meat is turned.

YIELD: 6 SERVINGS

Dilly Beef

1 (2–4 pound) boneless beef chuck roast, halved

1 (16 ounce) jar whole dill pickles, with brine

1 cup chili sauce

½ teaspoon minced garlic

½ teaspoon salt

½ teaspoon pepper

Place all ingredients in stoneware pot in oven at 275 degrees, or in slow cooker on low, for 8 to 9 hours. When cooked, discard pickles and shred beef into sauce. Serve on crisp rolls.

YIELD: 6–8 SANDWICHES

Garlic and Lemon Shrimp

1 pound medium raw shrimp, deveined and peeled

3 tablespoons lemon juice

3 cloves garlic, chopped

¼ cup extra virgin olive oil

½ teaspoon salt

¼ teaspoon pepper

½ cup grated Romano cheese

¾ cup fine bread crumbs

In large bowl, toss shrimp with lemon juice, garlic, olive oil, salt, and pepper. Add cheese and bread crumbs to coat shrimp evenly. Spread on foil-lined baking sheet and bake at 500 degrees until golden brown.

YIELD: 2–4 SERVINGS

Chicken Tetrazzini

1 cup shredded Parmesan cheese, divided

1 (10.5 ounce) can cream of mushroom soup

1 (10 ounce) jar refrigerated Alfredo sauce

1 (3.5 ounce) can sliced mushrooms, drained

½ cup slivered almonds, toasted

½ cup chicken broth

¼ cup dry cooking sherry

½ teaspoon salt

¼ teaspoon pepper

3 cups chopped cooked chicken

7 ounces vermicelli, cooked

Combine ½ cup Parmesan cheese and next eight ingredients in large bowl. Stir in chicken and pasta. Pour into lightly greased 8x11-inch casserole dish. Sprinkle with remaining ½ cup Parmesan and bake at 350 degrees for 30 minutes.

YIELD: 8 SERVINGS

Goulash

1 (12 ounce) package elbow
macaroni

1 pound ground beef

1 large onion, chopped

2 tablespoons butter

1 tablespoon olive oil

1 teaspoon salt

½ teaspoon pepper

1 teaspoon thyme

1½ cups milk

1 (10.5 ounce) can cream of celery
soup

1 (14.5 ounce) can diced tomatoes

½ cup canned diced tomatoes with
peppers

2 cups shredded mozzarella cheese

Cook macaroni according to package directions. Rinse and pour into
large mixing bowl. Brown beef and onion in butter and add, undrained,
to macaroni. In separate bowl, combine remaining ingredients (except
cheese) and stir into meat mixture. In large casserole dish, layer macaroni-
beef mixture and cheese several times. Bake at 350 degrees for 1 hour.

YIELD: 8 SERVINGS

Chicken in White Barbeque Sauce

2 cups mayonnaise

1 pint cider vinegar

½ cup honey

¼ teaspoon cayenne pepper

½ teaspoon prepared horseradish

1 teaspoon lemon juice

1 teaspoon salt

½ teaspoon pepper

Cut-up chicken for grilling

Place all ingredients (except chicken) in blender and blend for about 1 minute. Reserve and refrigerate 1 cup marinade for table sauce. (Serve warm with grilled chicken.) Pour remainder over chicken and marinate in refrigerator for several hours. Grill chicken for up to 1 hour, basting with marinade each time chicken is turned. Discard any remaining sauce that raw chicken marinated in.

YIELD: SAUCE FOR 1 CHICKEN

Chicken Taco Casserole

1 dozen corn tortillas

4 boneless, skinless chicken breasts, cooked and shredded

1 (10.5 ounce) can cream of chicken soup

1 (10.5 ounce) can cream of mushroom soup

1 soup can milk

½ cup minced onion

½ cup canned diced green chilies

Salt and pepper to taste

2 cups shredded sharp cheddar cheese

Sour cream for garnish

Sliced black olives for garnish

Cut tortillas in 2-inch pieces and toss with chicken in large casserole dish. Combine soups, milk, onion, green chilies, salt, and pepper. Pour over chicken and tortillas. Stir gently and refrigerate overnight. Bake at 325 degrees for 1 hour. Top with cheddar cheese and return to oven just until cheese is melted. Garnish with sour cream and black olives.

YIELD: 8 SERVINGS

Stuffed Bell Peppers with Quinoa

2 tablespoons olive oil

1 medium onion, finely chopped

2 stalks celery, diced

2 carrots, diced

1 dash cumin

2 teaspoons minced garlic

Any of the following "mix-ins": corn, black beans, chili beans, garbanzo beans, mushrooms, olives, diced tomato, diced zucchini, etc.

¾ cup raw quinoa

1 (14 ounce) can chicken broth

1½ cups shredded cheddar cheese

Salt and pepper to taste

4 bell peppers, any color

Add oil to large skillet and brown onion, celery, and carrot. Add cumin and garlic and sauté 1 minute longer. Stir in any "mix-ins" you like and cook 5 minutes longer. Stir in quinoa and broth. Cover and simmer for 20 minutes. Remove from heat and stir in cheese, salt, and pepper. Prepare bell peppers by cutting in half and removing seeds. Fill each half with hot mixture and place in baking dish. Pour small amount of chicken broth or juice from tomatoes around base of peppers and bake at 350 degrees, uncovered, for 20 minutes or until tops are browned.

YIELD: 8 SERVINGS

Chicken Marbella

8–10 boneless, skinless chicken breasts

2 teaspoons chopped garlic

½ cup chopped fresh oregano

1 teaspoon salt

½ teaspoon pepper

½ cup red wine vinegar

½ cup olive oil

1 cup pitted prunes or dried figs

¼ cup chopped fresh Italian parsley

½ cup pitted whole Spanish green olives

½ cup capers with 1 tablespoon juice

6 bay leaves

TOPPING:

1 cup brown sugar

1 cup white wine

In large bowl, toss chicken with remaining ingredients (except topping). Cover and refrigerate overnight. To bake, arrange chicken in single layer in one or two large baking pans. Spoon marinade evenly over chicken. Sprinkle with brown sugar and pour wine around base of chicken. Bake at 350 degrees for 1 hour. Remove bay leaves and serve with Nishiki rice or noodles.

YIELD: 8–10 SERVINGS

Swiss Steak on Rice Pilaf

1 large round steak, quartered

2 (10.5 ounce) cans cream of
   mushroom soup

1 soup can water

1 envelope onion soup mix

Salt and pepper to taste

RICE PILAF:

1 cup uncooked rice (not instant)

½ cup uncooked vermicelli, broken
   up

3 tablespoons butter

2 cups beef bouillon

¼ cup pine nuts

Salt and pepper to taste

Dump first five ingredients in slow cooker; stir, cover, and cook on low for
9 hours. Stir twice during that time. Sauté rice and vermicelli in butter
just until golden brown. Add bouillon. Stir and cover. Simmer for 10 to 15
minutes. Add pine nuts, salt, and pepper. Cook 5 to 10 minutes longer.

YIELD: 6–8 SERVINGS

Coffee Meatballs

¾ pound ground beef

¾ pound ground pork

1 egg, beaten

1 cup light cream

1½ cups coarse bread crumbs

¼ cup snipped parsley

1 teaspoon salt

1 generous dash each nutmeg, ginger, and pepper

3 tablespoons butter

½ cup chopped onion

2 tablespoons flour

1 tablespoon beef bouillon concentrate

1½ cups strong coffee

Egg noodles

1 jar Alfredo sauce

Place meat in large bowl and mix well with hands. Add egg, cream, bread crumbs, parsley, and seasonings. Blend well. Shape mixture into 3-inch meatballs and refrigerate for 2 hours. In large skillet, melt butter. Add meatballs and onion and brown. Remove from pan. Dissolve flour in mixture of bouillon and coffee and pour into hot skillet, stirring to make loose gravy. Return meatballs and onion to skillet, cover, and simmer gently for about 30 minutes, basting a couple of times. While meatballs simmer, cook egg noodles, drain, and add Alfredo sauce. Cover to keep warm. Serve meatballs over cheesy noodles.

YIELD: 6–8 SERVINGS

Pork Tenderloin

1 tablespoon dried minced onion

½ teaspoon garlic powder

½ teaspoon salt

¼ teaspoon pepper

¼ teaspoon ginger

½ teaspoon dry mustard

1½ cups soy sauce

½ cup dry cooking sherry

2–4 (1 pound) pork tenderloins

2 teaspoons cornstarch

2 tablespoons olive oil

Mix first eight ingredients together and pour into ziplock bag with meat. Refrigerate until ready to cook, up to two days. Drain off marinade into saucepan. Whisk in cornstarch and heat, stirring constantly, to make sauce. Sear meat in olive oil in heavy skillet. Turn to brown all sides. Set pan in 400-degree oven for 10 to 12 minutes. Remove from heat and cover. Let meat rest for 5 minutes before carving. Serve meat with sauce on side.

YIELD: 3 SERVINGS PER TENDERLOIN

Teriyaki Chicken

10–12 boneless, skinless chicken
  tenderloin strips

1 bottle teriyaki glaze

¼ cup red wine

3 tablespoons olive oil

Salt and pepper to taste

Pineapple tidbits, fresh or canned

Butter

Place chicken in ziplock bag with teriyaki glaze, wine, oil, salt, and pepper. Refrigerate for 2 hours. Drain off marinade and reserve. In large skillet, brown meat in small amount of oil. Remove to plate, tent with foil, and set aside. Pour marinade into pan with chicken drippings. Simmer slowly until slightly thickened, stirring to prevent burning. Return chicken to pan and heat through, topping with pineapple and pats of butter. Remove chicken, stir drippings to blend, and serve all over rice.

YIELD: 6 SERVINGS

Tilapia with Balsamic Sauce

4–6 tilapia filets

Flour

Salt and pepper to taste

4 tablespoons butter, divided

¼ cup balsamic vinegar

Pat fish dry and lightly dust with flour seasoned with salt and pepper. In large skillet, brown fish in 2 tablespoons butter. Set in warm oven to await sauce. In separate small skillet, cook remaining butter to a fragrant nutty brown, watching it carefully so it doesn't burn. Standing well back from potent steam, pour in balsamic vinegar. Bring mixture to simmer and let it reduce by half. When thick, pour over fish and serve with rice.

YIELD: 4–6 SERVINGS

Sangria Ham

2 cups brown sugar

1 bone-in butt portion ham

Whole cloves

2 cups sangria

1 cup pineapple juice

Pack brown sugar over exterior of ham. Stud with cloves. Place ham in roaster pan. Mix together sangria and pineapple juice and pour over meat. Bake at 325 degrees for 3 hours, basting every hour. Slice ham and pour cooking mixture juices over slices to serve.

YIELD: 12–15 SERVINGS

Slow Cooker Pork Roast

6 red potatoes, chunked

1 pork butt roast (about 3 pounds)

1 (12 ounce) can cola (Coke, Pepsi, etc.)

1 envelope onion soup mix

1 (10.5 ounce) can cream of mushroom soup

Salt and pepper to taste

8 carrots, sliced

Place red potatoes in slow cooker followed by roast. Dump in all other ingredients (except carrots) and cook on high for 6 hours. Put in carrots for last hour.

YIELD: 8 SERVINGS

Fettuccine Alfredo

1 cup butter

½ cup heavy cream

1 cup freshly grated Parmesan
    cheese

Salt and pepper to taste

½ teaspoon minced garlic

1 tablespoon fresh minced parsley

Fettuccine noodles, cooked

Optional: chicken or shrimp

In heavy saucepan, melt butter. Add cream and heat slowly, stirring and watching that mixture does not boil. Stir in remaining ingredients and heat through. Serve over fettuccine noodles and meat of your choice.

YIELD: 2 CUPS

Spicy Baby Back Ribs

2 racks baby back pork ribs

MEAT RUB:

1 teaspoon each chili powder, onion powder, Mrs. Dash seasoning, garlic powder, seasoned salt, salt, and pepper

½ cup hot sauce

½ cup honey

Rub spice mixture into meat and place in ziplock bag. Refrigerate for several hours. When ready to bake, combine hot sauce and honey. Pour over ribs. Place in covered Dutch oven or wrap in two layers of foil and place on baking sheet. Bake at 325 degrees for 3 hours. Just before serving, grill for 5 minutes on each side.

YIELD: 4 SERVINGS

On the tenth day of Christmas my true love sent to me. . .

Ten Salads a-Crunching

Christmas is most truly Christmas
when we celebrate it by giving the light
of love to those who need it most.

RUTH CARTER STAPLETON

Father, thank You for Your promise to love us,
teach us, correct us, and bless us! Thank You for
lighting our way, walking beside us, and encouraging
us as we serve and obey You—our joy, our peace,
and our constant resource. Amen.

*God said, "Look! I have given you every
seed-bearing plant throughout the earth
and all the fruit trees for your food."*

GENESIS 1:29 NLT

Broccoli Salad

3 cups chopped fresh broccoli

1 cup mayonnaise

½ cup red wine vinegar

½ cup sugar

¾ cup cooked, crumbled bacon

¾ cup raisins

¼ cup minced red onion

Salt and pepper to taste

Mix all ingredients together and refrigerate for 24 hours.

YIELD: 4 CUPS

Cold Salad

1 cup cooked corn

½ cup chopped celery

½ cup chopped cucumber

¼ cup chopped green onion

10 cherry tomatoes

5 slices bacon, fried crisp and crumbled

2 tablespoons olive oil

1 tablespoon lemon juice

1 tablespoon balsamic vinegar

1 tablespoon honey

Toss all ingredients together and serve immediately.

YIELD: 4 CUPS

Frozen Fruit Salad

1 (8 ounce) can crushed pineapple,
  with juice

2 eggs, beaten

½ cup sugar

¼ cup water

3 tablespoons lemon juice

1 dash salt

2 cups diced apple

½ cup walnuts or pecans

1 cup heavy whipping cream

In heavy saucepan, cook pineapple, eggs, sugar, water, lemon juice, and salt until thickened. Refrigerate for 1 hour. Stir in remaining ingredients and pour into 8-inch square dish. Freeze until 1 hour before serving. Cut into squares and garnish with mint leaf, maraschino cherries, or nuts if desired.

YIELD: 9 SERVINGS

Chicken Salad

2 cups chopped cooked chicken
  breast

1 tablespoon lemon juice

1 cup sliced celery

1 cup seedless green grapes, halved

¼ teaspoon salt

¼ teaspoon pepper

¼ teaspoon paprika

¾ cup mayonnaise

¼ cup slivered almonds, toasted

Combine all ingredients and chill well.

YIELD: 4 CUPS

Crab Salad

½ cup cream cheese, softened

2 tablespoons chopped green onion

2 tablespoons mayonnaise

1 tablespoon lime juice

1 dash each salt and pepper

1 teaspoon taco seasoning

6 ounces lump crabmeat

½ cup cooked corn

Combine first six ingredients. Fold in crab and corn. Refrigerate for 2 hours.

YIELD: 2 CUPS

Cranberry Rice Salad

⁂ ⁂ ⁂

1½ cups cooked white rice

½ cup cooked wild rice

½ cup dried cranberries

¼ cup chopped parsley

Salt and pepper to taste

2 tablespoons olive oil

1 tablespoon chopped green onions

¼ teaspoon ground cloves

Combine all ingredients. Store in refrigerator. Can be served warm or cold.

YIELD: 6 SERVINGS

Red Hot Applesauce Salad

⁂ ⁂ ⁂

½ cup red cinnamon candies

2 cups boiling water

1 (6 ounce) package lemon gelatin

16 ounces applesauce

1 dash salt

Whipped cream for garnish

Dissolve candies in boiling water and use to prepare gelatin according to package directions. Refrigerate for 30 minutes. Stir in applesauce and salt and refrigerate until set. Serve with dollop of whipped cream.

YIELD: 6 SERVINGS

Egg Salad

8 eggs

1 cup mayonnaise

1 teaspoon Dijon mustard

1 teaspoon red wine vinegar

2 tablespoons dried minced onion

1 teaspoon seasoned salt

½ teaspoon coarse ground pepper

½ teaspoon celery salt

¼ teaspoon paprika

1 teaspoon parsley flakes

¼ teaspoon garlic salt

Hard boil eggs. Remove shells and place eggs in large bowl. Chop finely with fork. Add remaining ingredients and stir well. Chill.

YIELD: 3 CUPS

Layered Salad

2 cups shredded iceberg lettuce

10 ounces fresh spinach leaves

4 hard-boiled eggs, chopped

1 bunch green onions, chopped

1 pound bacon, fried crisp and crumbled

1 (10 ounce) package frozen petite peas, thawed

1 cup shredded swiss cheese

Optional: chopped celery, chopped tomatoes

DRESSING:

1½ cups sour cream

1½ cups mayonnaise

2 teaspoons sugar

Salt and pepper to taste

Combine all dressing ingredients. Beginning with lettuce, layer ingredients in order given in 9x13-inch glass dish, spreading a little dressing between each set of layers. End with layer of dressing topped with swiss cheese. Cover and refrigerate for several hours.

YIELD: 10 SERVINGS

Ramen Noodle Salad

1 bag (or 1 small head) finely chopped cabbage

2 cups uncooked ramen noodles, slightly broken up

1 cup olive oil

½ cup vinegar

½ cup slivered almonds, toasted

Salt and pepper to taste

Toss all ingredients together and refrigerate for 4 hours.

YIELD: 5 CUPS

Pretzel Salad

¾ cup butter, melted

3 tablespoons sugar

2 cups crushed pretzels

1 (8 ounce) package cream cheese, softened

¾ cup sugar

1 (8 ounce) tub frozen whipped topping, thawed

2 small packages strawberry gelatin

2 cups boiling water

2 cups frozen unsweetened strawberries

1 cup crushed pineapple, drained

In large bowl, combine butter, 3 tablespoons sugar, and crushed pretzels. Press into 9x13-inch pan and bake at 350 degrees for 10 minutes. Cool completely. Whisk together cream cheese and ¾ cup sugar until well blended. Fold in whipped topping. Spread evenly over cooled crust. In separate bowl, combine strawberry gelatin and boiling water. Stir to dissolve. Add fruit and refrigerate until cool and thick but not yet set. Pour over cream cheese and spread evenly. Allow to set in refrigerator for 4 hours.

YIELD: 12 SERVINGS

Pink Cherry Salad

1 (20 ounce) can cherry pie filling

1 small can crushed pineapple, drained

1 (14 ounce) can sweetened condensed milk

1 cup cottage cheese

1 dash salt

2 drops red food coloring

1 (16 ounce) tub frozen whipped topping, thawed, or 2 cups stiffly whipped cream

Combine all ingredients except whipped topping. When well blended, fold in whipped topping. Refrigerate for at least 2 hours.

YIELD: 3 CUPS

Chow Mein Noodle Salad

1 cup frozen peas, cooked al dente

1 cup shredded carrots

1 tablespoon dried minced onion

1 small can tuna

1 tablespoon Worcestershire sauce

½ cup mayonnaise

2 hard-boiled eggs, diced

2 cups chow mein noodles

Combine first six ingredients and chill. Just before serving, add eggs and noodles.

YIELD: 4 CUPS

Kidney Bean Salad

2 hard-boiled eggs, chopped

¼ cup chopped celery

1 medium onion, minced

2½ cups canned kidney beans,
  drained and rinsed

½ teaspoon salt

¼ teaspoon pepper

2 tablespoons sugar

2 tablespoons vinegar

¼ cup mayonnaise

2 tablespoons heavy cream

Combine eggs, celery, and onion. Gently toss in beans. In separate bowl, combine remaining ingredients to make creamy dressing. Pour over eggs and vegetable mixture. Stir gently and chill well.

YIELD: 6 SERVINGS

Mandarin Orange Salad

2 small packages orange gelatin

1 cup boiling water

2 cups orange sherbet

1 (15 ounce) can mandarin
  oranges, drained

1 cup heavy cream, whipped

Dissolve gelatin in boiling water. Stir in sherbet until melted. Chill until thick and cool but not set; then fold in oranges and whipped cream. Pour into mold or serving bowl and let set in refrigerator for 2 hours.

YIELD: 8 SERVINGS

German Potato Salad

4 cups diced cooked potatoes, hot

1 tablespoon chopped fresh parsley

½ ring kielbasa sausage, sliced and diced

½ cup chopped celery

1 medium onion, chopped

2 tablespoons vegetable oil

1 tablespoon flour

1 teaspoon salt

½ teaspoon pepper

⅓ cup sugar

⅓ cup vinegar

⅔ cup water

Place potatoes and parsley in large bowl and set aside. Brown meat, celery, and onion in hot oil. Remove from pan and drain on paper towel. Add to potatoes. Add flour to drippings in skillet, whisking quickly. Add salt, pepper, sugar, vinegar, and water. Cook and stir until thickened. Pour hot mixture over potatoes, meat, and vegetables. Serve hot.

Yield: 6–8 servings

Coleslaw

4 cups finely shredded cabbage

2 carrots, shredded

½ cup sour cream

¼ cup cider vinegar

3 tablespoons sugar

1 teaspoon salt

½ teaspoon pepper

1 dash dry mustard

Place cabbage and carrots in large bowl. Mix together remaining ingredients, blending well. Pour over cabbage mixture, stir gently, and chill.

YIELD: 6 SERVINGS

Russian Cucumber Salad

4 medium cucumbers

1 tablespoon salt, divided

2 tablespoons vinegar

1 quart buttermilk

Peel cucumbers and cut into thin slices. Sprinkle with 1½ teaspoons salt and let stand for 5 minutes. Whisk vinegar and remaining salt into buttermilk. Drain cucumbers and add to milk mixture.

YIELD: 3 CUPS

Fancy Tuna Salad

2 cups canned tuna, drained

1 cup frozen peas, cooked al dente and cooled

½ cup diced celery

½ cup diced red onion

¼ teaspoon paprika

¼ teaspoon salt

1 dash pepper

1 cup grape halves

½ cup chopped walnuts

1½ cups mayonnaise

In large bowl, combine first seven ingredients. Fold in grapes, walnuts, and mayonnaise. Serve with crispy crackers or toasted bread, lettuce, and tomato.

YIELD: 6 SERVINGS

Carrot Salad

¼ cup raisins

1 cup boiling water

2 cups shredded carrots

2 tablespoons lemon juice

4 teaspoons mayonnaise

1 dash salt

Soak raisins in boiling water for 30 minutes. Drain well. Stir in remaining ingredients and refrigerate for 2 hours.

YIELD: 3 CUPS

On the eleventh day of Christmas my true love sent to me. . .

Eleven Sides a-Steaming

It is Christmas every time you let God love others through you. . .yes, it is Christmas every time you smile at your brother and offer him your hand.

MOTHER TERESA

Jesus, precious Son of God, You came to
earth as a child, beloved by the human parents
entrusted with Your upbringing. Help us to train
up our children, as Mary and Joseph did,
in the way pleasing to You. Amen.

*"Open your mouth wide,
and I will fill it with good things."*

PSALM 81:10 NLT

Spinach Casserole

6 cups chopped fresh spinach

1 cup sour cream

¾ envelope onion soup mix

1 cup shredded sharp cheddar cheese

Cook spinach until limp and drain well. Place in casserole dish and top with sour cream and soup mix. Stir and top with cheese. Bake uncovered at 350 degrees for 20 minutes.

YIELD: 4 SERVINGS

Corn Pudding

2 eggs, beaten

1 cup whole milk

½ cup fine bread crumbs

2 cups corn

3 tablespoons butter, melted

½ teaspoon salt

¼ teaspoon pepper

1 tablespoon sugar

1 teaspoon dried minced onion

Combine eggs, milk, and bread crumbs. Add remaining ingredients and pour into greased 9x11-inch baking dish. Bake at 350 degrees for 45 minutes.

YIELD: 8 SERVINGS

Scalloped Pineapple

2 cups crushed butter-flavored crackers

1 cup butter, melted

2 cups sugar

3 eggs, beaten

2 (20 ounce) cans pineapple chunks, drained

1 cup milk

½ teaspoon salt

1 cup shredded cheddar cheese

Combine crackers, butter, sugar, and eggs. Stir pineapple into milk and salt. Fold in cheese. Add to cracker mixture and pour into greased 9x11-inch baking dish. Bake at 350 degrees for 40 minutes.

YIELD: 8 SERVINGS

Sweet Potato Casserole

6 cups cooked and mashed
   sweet potatoes

1 cup sugar

1 teaspoon salt

4 eggs, beaten

½ cup butter, melted

1 cup milk

1 teaspoon cinnamon

TOPPING:

  1 cup brown sugar

  ⅓ cup flour

  1 cup chopped nuts

  ⅓ cup butter

Mix together first seven ingredients and pour into greased 9x13-inch pan. Combine topping ingredients and crumble evenly over sweet potato mixture. Bake at 350 degrees for 1 hour.

YIELD: 10 SERVINGS

Creamed Corn

1 (16 ounce) package frozen corn

8 ounces heavy whipping cream

2 tablespoons butter, melted

1½ tablespoons flour

½ teaspoon salt

¼ teaspoon pepper

2 tablespoons sugar

½ cup shaved Gruyère cheese

In heavy saucepan, heat corn and whipping cream. Do not allow to boil. Make rue of melted butter, flour, salt, pepper, and sugar and whisk briskly into cream mixture until thickened. Pour into casserole dish and top with cheese. Bake at 400 degrees for about 3 minutes or until cheese is melted.

YIELD: 8 SERVINGS

Party Spuds

4 cups partially thawed hash browns

1 cup sour cream

1 (10.75 ounce) can cream of chicken soup

2 tablespoons dried minced onion

1 teaspoon salt

½ teaspoon pepper

2 cups shredded cheddar cheese

½ cup butter, melted

1 cup crushed saltine crackers

Mix together first seven ingredients and pour into greased 9x13-inch baking dish. Drizzle butter over all and sprinkle crackers on top. Bake at 350 degrees for 50 minutes.

YIELD: 10 SERVINGS

Peas in Browned Butter

3 cups frozen peas

½ cup minced onion

1 teaspoon salt

¼ teaspoon pepper

1 teaspoon sugar

½ cup water

2 tablespoons butter

Cook first five ingredients in ½ cup water. Drain. In separate small skillet, melt butter. Stir and cook until lightly brown in color. Pour over drained vegetables and serve immediately.

YIELD: 6 SERVINGS

Sweet-and-Sour Red Cabbage

1 tablespoon salt

⅔ cup sugar

1 cup water

⅓ cup red wine vinegar

⅓ cup cider vinegar

8 cups shredded red cabbage

In large Dutch oven, combine salt, sugar, water, and vinegars. Bring to boil and add cabbage. Cover and reduce heat to simmer for 35 minutes. Serve hot or cold.

YIELD: 6 SERVINGS

Broccoli Rice Casserole

4 cups frozen chopped broccoli

2 tablespoons butter, melted

½ cup chopped onion

1 cup uncooked instant rice

¼ cup milk

1 (10.5 ounce) can cream of celery soup

1 soup can water

1 (8 ounce) jar processed cheese sauce

Combine all ingredients in greased casserole dish and bake covered at 350 degrees for 45 minutes.

YIELD: 6 SERVINGS

Whole Buttered Baby Beets

20–25 tiny beets

1 teaspoon salt

½ teaspoon pepper

3 tablespoons butter

Remove greens and wash beets well. Cook with salt and pepper until tender, about 30 minutes. Remove from heat. Drain and lightly peel off any tough outer skin of beets. Pour into serving dish and toss with butter.

YIELD: 6 SERVINGS

Corn Bread Stuffing

2 cups unseasoned dried stuffing
  cubes

2 cups coarsely crumbled corn
  bread

½ cup chopped onion

½ cup chopped celery

½ cup chopped green pepper

½ cup butter

2 teaspoons crushed sage

2½ teaspoons salt

1 teaspoon pepper

1½ cups turkey broth or canned
  chicken broth

Combine stuffing cubes and corn bread in large bowl. In skillet, lightly
brown vegetables in butter. Stir in seasonings. Pour over stuffing and corn
bread mixture and toss to blend well. Add broth and pour into greased
baking dish. Reserve some for turkey if you wish. Bake at 350 degrees for
45 minutes.

YIELD: 6–8 SERVINGS

Green Beans and Water Chestnuts

4 slices bacon, fried crisp and crumbled

2 (15.5 ounce) cans french-cut green beans, drained

½ teaspoon crushed garlic

1 (8 ounce) can sliced water chestnuts, drained

Salt and pepper to taste

After frying bacon and removing it to cool, add beans and garlic to hot drippings and stir-fry for 1 minute. Add sliced water chestnuts and toss for another minute to coat. Season with salt and pepper. Serve garnished with crumbled bacon.

YIELD: 4 SERVINGS

Lima Bean Confit

4 slices bacon, fried crisp and crumbled

1 teaspoon minced garlic

1 dash dried oregano

1 teaspoon salt

¼ teaspoon pepper

4 cups frozen lima beans

⅓ cup grated Parmesan cheese

Fry bacon and remove to paper towel to drain and cool. Add garlic, oregano, salt, and pepper to bacon drippings and cook for 1 minute. Add lima beans and toss; simmer, covered, for 5 minutes. Pour into serving dish, top with cheese and crumbled bacon, and serve immediately.

YIELD: 4–6 SERVINGS

Cranberry Relish

1 (16 ounce) bag fresh cranberries

1 apple, finely diced

1 (15 ounce) can mandarin oranges, drained

1 cup sugar

2 tablespoons finely grated orange peel

½ teaspoon salt

½ cup chopped pecans

In large saucepan, cook cranberries in *water* until soft. Cool. Mix in remaining ingredients. Refrigerate for two days before serving.

YIELD: 2 CUPS

Creamed Onions

3 cups canned baby onions, drained

4 tablespoons butter

4 tablespoons flour

1 cup whole milk

1 cup half-and-half

1 teaspoon salt

½ teaspoon pepper

Place onions in greased baking dish. In heavy saucepan, whisk together remaining ingredients and cook, stirring, until thickened. Pour over onions and bake at 350 degrees for 15 minutes.

YIELD: 6 SERVINGS

Copper Carrots

3 pounds carrots, sliced

1 cup vinegar

1 cup sugar

1 teaspoon dry mustard

½ cup vegetable oil

1 tablespoon Worcestershire sauce

1 tablespoon tomato paste

1 small can diced tomatoes

½ cup diced green pepper

Salt and pepper to taste

Boil carrots until al dente. Drain. Combine next six ingredients and toss with carrots. Pour into buttered baking dish and top with tomatoes and green pepper. Add salt and pepper and bake uncovered at 325 degrees for 20 minutes.

YIELD: 8 SERVINGS

Broccoli and Cauliflower Bake

1½ cups broccoli florets

1½ cups cauliflower florets

⅓ cup mayonnaise

2 tablespoons lemon juice

1 (10.5 ounce) can cream of
mushroom soup

1 tablespoon diced pimentos

1 cup melted pasteurized process
cheese spread

Salt and pepper to taste

½ cup crushed butter-flavored
crackers

Cook broccoli and cauliflower in small amount of salted *water* in covered saucepan. Florets should remain firm. In separate bowl, combine mayonnaise, lemon juice, soup, and pimentos. Pour melted cheese over all; season with salt and pepper and sprinkle with crackers. Bake covered at 350 degrees for 25 minutes.

YIELD: 8 SERVINGS

Hearty Baked Beans

2 (15 ounce) cans Great Northern beans, drained and rinsed

2 tablespoons dried minced onion

½ teaspoon salt

½ teaspoon pepper

½ cup ketchup

2 tablespoons molasses

½ cup brown sugar

1 teaspoon mustard

2 teaspoons cider vinegar

4 slices bacon, fried crisp and crumbled

In large bowl, stir together all ingredients. Pour into baking dish and bake at 350 degrees for 30 minutes or until bubbly.

Yield: 6 servings

Mashed Potatoes Especial

2 pounds white potatoes, peeled
  and quartered

½ teaspoon salt

½ teaspoon pepper

⅓ cup half-and-half

⅓ cup whole milk

½ cup butter

1 tablespoon balsamic vinegar

Boil potatoes until very soft. Drain and add remaining ingredients. Mash by hand, adding more milk if potatoes are too dry.

YIELD: 8 SERVINGS

On the twelfth day of Christmas my true love sent to me. . .

Twelve Soups a-Simmering

Christmas waves a
magic wand over this world,
and behold, everything is
softer and more beautiful.

NORMAN VINCENT PEALE

Dear Father, help me to balance my life well.
Be the permanent heart of my home. Warm by Your
presence every activity. . .my work, worship, rest,
and play. From my rising up each morning to
my lying down at night, Lord, remind me
of Your nearness! Amen.

*You cause grass to grow for the livestock
and plants for people to use. You allow
them to produce food from the earth.*

PSALM 104:14 NLT

Prime Rib and Barley Soup

Leftover bones and meat from prime rib roast

2 quarts water

2 teaspoons salt

1 onion, diced

2 tablespoons beef stock concentrate

1 cup barley, cooked

1 tablespoon butter

1 (14.5 ounce) can diced tomatoes

2 carrots, sliced

½ cup diced celery

1 cup frozen green beans

1 teaspoon celery salt

1 teaspoon salt

1 teaspoon pepper

½ teaspoon paprika

Place bones and meat in salted water and simmer for 2 hours or until meat pulls away from bones easily. Separate fat and bones from meat and discard. Pour remaining broth through sieve and combine with meat. Brown onion and add along with remaining ingredients to broth and meat. Simmer for 30 minutes.

YIELD: 3 QUARTS

Santa Fe Soup

1 onion, diced

1 tablespoon vegetable oil

3 cups chopped cooked chicken
breast

2 (15 ounce) cans black beans

2 (11 ounce) cans white corn

2 (14.5 ounce) cans diced tomatoes

1 (15 ounce) jar salsa

1 envelope dry ranch dressing mix

2 envelopes taco seasoning mix

2 cups chicken stock

Shredded cheese, sour cream,
tortilla chips, black olives, etc.
for garnish

Tortilla chips

In large soup pot, brown onion in oil. Add remaining ingredients (except garnishes) and stir. Simmer for 20 to 30 minutes. Garnish as desired and serve with tortilla chips.

YIELD: 4 SERVINGS

French Onion Soup

2 onions, roughly chopped

¼ cup butter (no substitutes)

1 quart beef stock

1 tablespoon beef stock
concentrate

Salt and pepper to taste

4 baguette slices, toasted

1 cup shaved Gruyère cheese

In large skillet, sauté onions in butter until slightly brown and tender. Add beef stock, beef stock concentrate, salt, and pepper. Simmer uncovered for 1 hour or until reduced by one-third. To serve, place one baguette slice in each serving bowl. Pour in hot soup and top generously with cheese. Immediately place bowls on jelly roll pan and put under broiler to melt and brown cheese.

YIELD: 4 SERVINGS

Corn Chowder

½ pound bacon

1 onion, chopped

1 cup chopped celery

1 cup shredded carrots

½ cup flour

5½ cups whole milk

2 (14.75 ounce) cans cream-style corn

1 (15.5 ounce) can whole kernel corn

2 cups diced cooked potatoes

Salt and pepper to taste

Chopped red bell pepper, fresh parsley, paprika, and crumbled bacon for garnish

In skillet, fry bacon until crisp. Remove and let drain and cool. Discard all but 4 tablespoons bacon drippings. Add onion, celery, and carrots to drippings and sauté until tender. In separate bowl, whisk flour into milk. Stir into vegetable mixture. Add corn, potatoes, salt, and pepper. Heat thoroughly. Garnish with red pepper, snips of parsley, dash of paprika, and crumbled bacon.

YIELD: 6 SERVINGS

Turkey Chili

2 pounds ground turkey

1 large onion, chopped

2 cloves garlic, minced

1 (15 ounce) can Great Northern beans, drained and rinsed

2 quarts chicken broth

1 (15 ounce) can black beans, drained and rinsed

2 tablespoons chopped jalapeño pepper

1 small can green chilies

1 (14.5 ounce) can diced tomatoes

2 tablespoons cumin

Salt and pepper to taste

Shredded Mexican cheese blend and tortilla chips for garnish

In large soup pot, brown turkey and onion together. Add remaining ingredients except cheese and chips. Simmer on low heat for 2 hours, stirring occasionally. Serve with shredded cheese and tortilla chips.

YIELD: 8 SERVINGS

Cream of Zucchini Soup

4 medium zucchini, quartered and sliced

4 cups chicken broth

8 green onions, chopped

Salt and pepper to taste

½ teaspoon dill weed

2 (8 ounce) packages cream cheese, softened

1 cup sour cream

Chives and paprika for garnish

In saucepan, combine zucchini, chicken broth, green onions, and seasonings. Cook for 20 minutes or until soft. In blender, process cream cheese and sour cream until smooth. Add cooled zucchini mixture, 1 cup at a time, blending until smooth. Pour into large bowl and refrigerate overnight or until very cold. Serve warm or cold with garnish of chives and paprika.

YIELD: 8 SERVINGS

Split Pea Soup

1 leftover ham bone with some
   meat attached

2 quarts water

1 small onion, chopped

1 stalk celery, chopped

2 medium carrots, chopped

2 cups frozen peas

1 small can tomato puree

¼ teaspoon ginger

Salt and pepper to taste

½ cup whole milk

Sour cream and crumbled bacon
   for garnish

In large soup pot, simmer ham bone in water for 2 to 3 hours or until meat pulls away from bone easily. Discard fat and gristle, leaving meat and bone. Add vegetables, puree, and seasonings. Simmer until vegetables are soft. Remove ham bone and let soup cool. Put mixture (meat and veggies) in blender and blend until smooth. Return to pot and add milk. Reheat and garnish with sour cream and crumbled bacon.

YIELD: 8 SERVINGS

Butternut Squash Bisque

1 large butternut squash, halved,
    seeded, and baked

½ cup butter

Salt and pepper to taste

1 small onion, diced

4 cups chicken stock

1 teaspoon celery salt

1 teaspoon paprika

1 cup heavy cream

Sour cream and crumbled bacon
    for garnish

After baking, scoop out cooled squash into large soup pot. Add next six
ingredients. Simmer for 20 minutes. Cool. Put mixture in blender and
blend until smooth. Return to pot and add heavy cream. Reheat, but do
not allow to boil. Garnish with sour cream and bacon.

YIELD: 8 SERVINGS

Minestrone

- 1 large onion, chopped
- 1 tablespoon vegetable oil
- 8 cups beef stock
- 2 carrots, chopped
- 2 large white potatoes, cooked and mashed
- 1 bag fresh spinach
- 1 (15 ounce) can pinto beans
- 1 (14.5 ounce) can diced tomatoes
- 1 cup shell pasta, cooked al dente
- ½ teaspoon dried basil or 2–3 fresh basil leaves
- 1 teaspoon chopped garlic
- Salt and pepper to taste

In soup pot, brown onion in oil. Add beef stock, carrots, and potatoes. Simmer just until carrots are cooked but firm, about 20 minutes. Stir in remaining ingredients and simmer 30 minutes longer.

YIELD: 8 SERVINGS

Dr. Smiley Soup

1 cup uncooked rice (not instant)

2 quarts chicken stock

1 tablespoon black pepper

1 teaspoon salt

½ teaspoon celery salt

½ teaspoon paprika

4 eggs, well beaten

2 tablespoons chopped green onion
for garnish

In large soup pot, prepare rice using chicken stock as liquid. Add remaining soup stock and spices. Simmer for 20 minutes until rice is nearly breaking up. Gradually pour in eggs while stirring in wide circular motion with whisk. Eggs will cook immediately in shreds. Garnish each serving with chopped green onion.

YIELD: 6 SERVINGS

Broccoli Cheese Soup

1 cup chopped onion

2 tablespoons butter

4 cups chicken stock

3 cups broccoli florets, cooked

½ teaspoon garlic powder

Salt and pepper to taste

2 cups half-and-half

2 cups cubed American cheese

In large soup pot, sauté onion in butter. Add chicken stock and simmer for 5 minutes. Add broccoli, garlic powder, salt, and pepper and continue to simmer 5 minutes longer. Add half-and-half and cheese and let soup heat and melt cheese over very low heat. Soup will be chunky. For creamier soup, blend broccoli in blender with 1 cup stock before adding to soup. If soup is too thick, add milk to desired consistency.

YIELD: 8 SERVINGS

Cream of Mushroom Soup

3 cups finely diced shiitake mushrooms

½ cup chopped leeks

1 teaspoon minced garlic

1 tablespoon butter

2 tablespoons flour

4 cups milk, divided

2 tablespoons dry cooking sherry

1 tablespoon chopped fresh parsley

2 tablespoons chicken stock concentrate

¼ teaspoon thyme

Salt and pepper to taste

In large soup pot, sauté mushrooms, leeks, and garlic in butter until tender. In small bowl, dissolve flour in 1 cup milk. Add to sautéed vegetables along with remaining 3 cups milk and rest of ingredients, stirring constantly over medium heat as soup thickens. Simmer on very low heat for 30 minutes. For creamier soup, run cooked vegetables through blender before adding liquid.

YIELD: 8 SERVINGS

Turkey and Wild Rice Soup

1 quart chicken broth

1 cup wild rice, cooked

½ cup chopped green onion

½ cup butter

½ cup flour

Salt and pepper to taste

¼ teaspoon poultry seasoning

2 cups half-and-half

1 tablespoon chopped pimento for garnish

In large soup pot, combine chicken broth, rice, and green onion. In separate pan, melt butter and whisk in flour and seasonings. Gradually add half-and-half. Cook, stirring constantly, until smooth. Pour into broth and rice mixture and reheat. Add garnish.

YIELD: 6 SERVINGS

Shrimp and Veggie Gumbo

1 cup chopped onion

1 cup chopped green pepper

½ cup chopped celery

1 teaspoon crushed garlic

2 tablespoons vegetable oil

1 bay leaf, crumbled

Salt and pepper to taste

1 (14.5 ounce) can diced tomatoes

1 quart chicken broth

2 cups frozen okra, thawed

½ pound shrimp, cooked, tails off

3½ cups cooked rice

Chopped fresh parsley for garnish

In Dutch oven, sauté onion, green pepper, celery, and garlic in oil, stirring frequently, until vegetables are tender. Add bay leaf and salt and pepper. Mash tomatoes until pulpy and add to chicken broth. Stir in okra. Simmer, covered, for 15 minutes. Add shrimp and reheat. Spoon over rice and sprinkle with parsley.

YIELD: 8 CUPS

Fish Chowder

3 tablespoons butter

1 onion, sliced

2 cups diced cooked potatoes

2 cups hot water

1 teaspoon salt

½ teaspoon pepper

½ teaspoon celery salt

1 tablespoon parsley flakes

2 dashes paprika

1 pound fish filets, baked

1 (12 ounce) can evaporated milk

Melt butter in heavy saucepan and sauté onion. Add potatoes, water, and seasonings. Simmer for 10 minutes. Add fish in chunky crumbles. Stir in milk and reheat.

YIELD: 6 SERVINGS

Creamy Tomato Soup

2 (16 ounce) cans tomato sauce

1 teaspoon salt

½ teaspoon pepper

1 teaspoon parsley flakes

1 teaspoon celery salt

½ teaspoon cumin

1 cup half-and-half

In large soup pot, combine all ingredients except half-and-half. Simmer on low for 1 hour. Stir in half-and-half and reheat, but do not boil.

YIELD: 4 SERVINGS

Sausage and Tortellini Soup

3 carrots, shredded

1 onion, diced

1 teaspoon minced garlic

2 tablespoons butter

6 cups chicken broth

1 pound Italian sausage, browned and drained

1 pound ground beef, browned and drained

1 teaspoon basil

1 teaspoon oregano

2 (14.5 ounce) cans crushed tomatoes

3 small zucchini, cut in thick slices

2 packages tortellini pasta

Grated Parmesan cheese for garnish

Sauté carrots, onion, and garlic in butter. In separate large soup pot, combine broth, meats, seasonings, tomatoes, and sautéed vegetables. Simmer for 10 minutes. Add zucchini and pasta. Simmer for additional 20 minutes. Garnish with Parmesan.

YIELD: 8–10 SERVINGS

Corny Clam Chowder

1 onion, chopped

2 tablespoons butter

2 cups frozen corn, thawed

1 cup mashed potatoes

Salt and pepper to taste

1 teaspoon celery salt

½ teaspoon paprika

1 tablespoon chopped fresh parsley

1 cup chicken broth

2 cups whole milk

2 cups half-and-half

2 cups canned clams, with juice

Brown onion in butter. Add next seven ingredients and simmer for 15 minutes. Add milk and half-and-half, stirring constantly. Continue to simmer on low heat for additional 8 minutes. Add clams and simmer 2 minutes longer or until well heated.

YIELD: 8 SERVINGS

Hearty Ham and Bean Soup

* * *

2 cups milk

1 cup half-and-half

2 cups Great Northern beans, unrinsed

1 cup chopped ham

½ cup chopped celery

1 tablespoon chopped fresh parsley

Salt and pepper to taste

In heavy saucepan, heat milk and half-and-half to hot, but not boiling. Add beans, ham, celery, parsley, and seasonings. Simmer on low for 30 minutes.

YIELD: 6 SERVINGS

Taco Soup

* * *

1 pound ground beef

½ cup chopped onion

1 (14.5 ounce) can diced tomatoes

1 (15 ounce) can kidney beans, drained but unrinsed

1 (15 ounce) can chili beans, drained but unrinsed

1 (8 ounce) can tomato sauce

1 envelope taco seasoning mix

1 cup beef broth

Brown beef and onions together. Drain and return to pan. Add remaining ingredients (except cheese and chips) and simmer for 15 minutes. Serve with shredded cheese and tortilla chips.

YIELD: 8 SERVINGS

Index

APPETIZERS

BEVERAGES

BREADS

BREAKFAST DISHES

CANDIES

COOKIES

DESSERTS

KIDS' RECIPES

MAIN DISHES

SALADS

SIDES

SOUPS